W9-AGF-520

Super Toys & Games from Paper

F. Virginia Walter

A Sterling/Tamos Book

Sterling Publishing Co., Inc. New York

A Sterling/Tamos Book

First paperback edition published in 1994 by
Sterling Publishing Company, Inc.
387 Park Avenue South, New York, N.Y. 10016
and
TAMOS Books Inc.
300 Wales Avenue, Winnipeg, MB, Canada R2M 2S9

© 1993 by F. Virginia Walter

10 9 8 7 6 5 4 3 2 1

Distributed in Canada by Sterling Publishing
% Canadian Manda Group, P.O. Box 920, Station U
Toronto, Ontario, Canada M8Z 5P9
Distributed in Great Britain and Europe by Cassell PLC
Villiers House, 41/47 Strand, London WC2N 5JE, England
Distributed in Australia by Capricorn Link (Australia) Pty Ltd.
P.O. Box 6651, Baulkham Hills, Business Centre, NSW 2153, Australia

Illustrations Teddy Cameron Long
Photography Walter Kaiser, Custom Images Ltd., Wpg
Design A. O. Osen

Library of Congress Cataloging-in-Publication Data
Walter, F. Virginia.
    Super toys & games from paper / F. Virginia Walter
        p.   cm.
    Includes index.
    Summary: Provides instructions for making games and
toys using paper and paper products.
        ISBN 1-895569-06-0
    1. Paper work--Juvenile literature. 2. Paper toys--Juvenile
literature. 3. Games--Juvenile literature. [1. Paper work.
2. Paper toy making. 3. Toy making. 4. Handicraft. 5. Games.]
I. Long, Teddy Cameron. II. Title.   III. Title: Super toys and
games from paper.
TT870.W28   1993
745.592--dc20
                                                    93-3161
                                                    CIP
                                                    AC

Canadian Cataloging-in-Publication Data
Walter, F. Virginia, 1935–
    Super toys & games from paper
    ISBN 1-895569-06-0
    1. Paper toy making. 2. Paper work. I. Long, Teddy
Cameron. II. Title
TT174.5.P3W34 1993   745.592   C93-098008-5

Printed in Hong Kong

Sterling ISBN 1-895569-06-0 Trade
            1-895569-28-1 Paper

Table of Contents

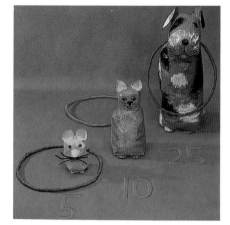

Introduction

Making toys from paper is an easy and fun-filled way to create delightful play material for children. Doll houses, dolls, teddy bears, sailboats, airplanes, farm animals, puppets, games, and even zoo animals take shape from used newspaper, cardboard tubes, and paper bags that you have around the house. Add some glue and a little paint and your special toys are ready to delight youngsters for many hours of play.

You don't need any special equipment. The finished toys are sturdy and the projects are simple and inexpensive to make. Even pre-schoolers can share in the activities. Some projects can be made by the children themselves; others require a little guidance from teacher or parent to help along the way. A group project is fun to do and many busy hands soon put everything in place. Act out a favorite nursery rhyme such as *The Three Little Pigs* or make up your own play with theater and puppets. This hands-on approach for making and doing allows children to use their imaginations and create the kinds of toys that appeal to their age and interest groups. Make the projects on a rainy day at home or have fun in the classroom, nursery school, or community center. Please be sure that small children use blunt end scissors and have help with sharp knives.

Remember, when you make toys and crafts from paper you are recycling the product from our trees and giving it a longer life. Used newspapers, paper bags, and cardboard tubes destined for the garbage can be used again to provide satisfaction and pleasure for everyone.

Games
&
Things

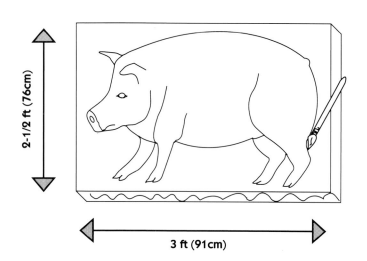

2-1/2 ft (76cm)

3 ft (91cm)

Pin the Tail on the Pig

Cut a piece of cardboard from a large box 2-1/2 ft by 3 ft (76cm x 91cm). Draw a pig without a tail. Indicate the winning spot with a bump or X.
Paint and shellac.

Wrap the end of a chenille stem around a push pin. Curl the rest of the chenille stem into a corkscrew. Number the tails by writing on the push pins with an indelible marker.

To play the game, blindfold the children one at a time, turn them around once, position the child facing the pig board, and let each attempt to place a tail on the correct spot.

Kick Ball

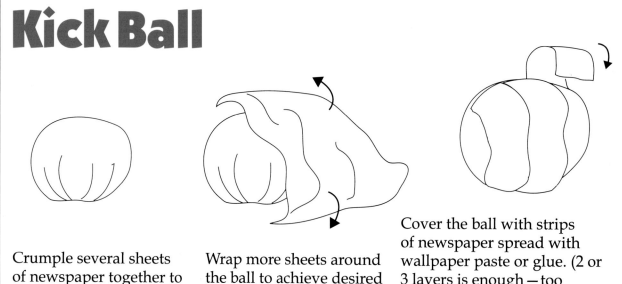

Crumple several sheets of newspaper together to form a large ball.

Wrap more sheets around the ball to achieve desired size. Tape loose edges.

Cover the ball with strips of newspaper spread with wallpaper paste or glue. (2 or 3 layers is enough—too many layers will make the ball too hard.) Paint and shellac.

Golf Clubs

Cut a 1/2 in (1.3cm) wooden dowel into 2 ft (61cm) lengths. Crumple sheets of newspaper into rectangles and tape to one end of each dowel, as shown. Fold some into rectangular shapes for irons, and others into rounded shapes for woods. Tape. Wrap more crumpled newspaper around the other end of each dowel to form a handle. Tape in place.

Cut many long strips of newspaper. Spread glue or wallpaper paste on strips and wrap them around the entire golf club. When dry, paint and shellac.

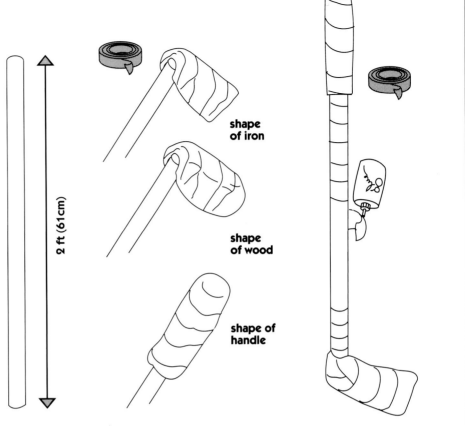

2 ft (61cm)

shape of iron

shape of wood

shape of handle

Golf Balls

Crumple half a sheet of newspaper into a tight ball. Wrap with strips of newspaper spread with wallpaper paste or glue. When dry, paint and shellac.

Golf Bag

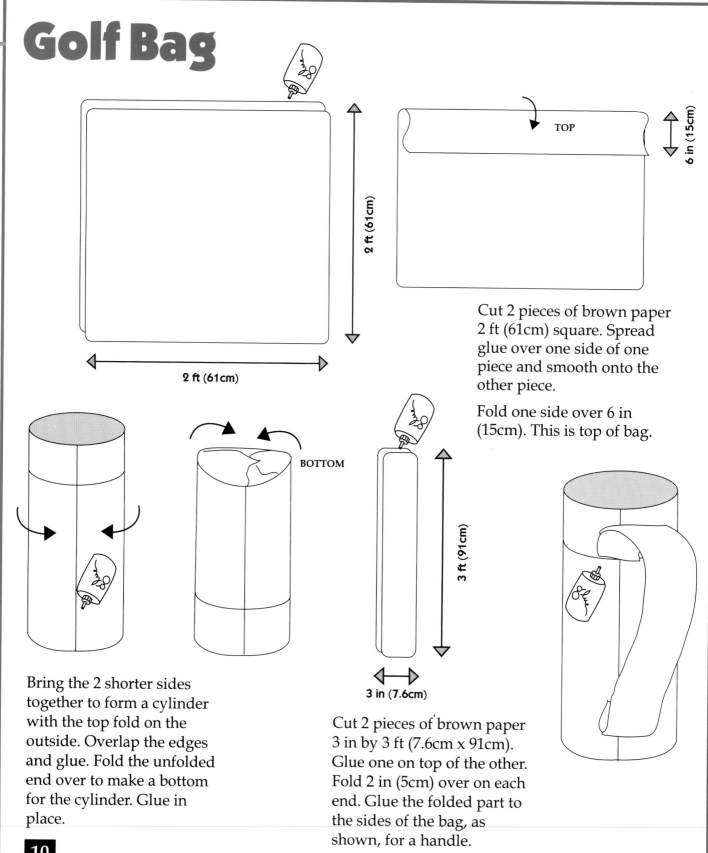

2 ft (61cm)

2 ft (61cm)

TOP

6 in (15cm)

Cut 2 pieces of brown paper 2 ft (61cm) square. Spread glue over one side of one piece and smooth onto the other piece.

Fold one side over 6 in (15cm). This is top of bag.

BOTTOM

3 ft (91cm)

3 in (7.6cm)

Bring the 2 shorter sides together to form a cylinder with the top fold on the outside. Overlap the edges and glue. Fold the unfolded end over to make a bottom for the cylinder. Glue in place.

Cut 2 pieces of brown paper 3 in by 3 ft (7.6cm x 91cm). Glue one on top of the other. Fold 2 in (5cm) over on each end. Glue the folded part to the sides of the bag, as shown, for a handle.

Hoop Toss Game

Dog

Spread glue on the outside of one brown paper grocery bag and press inside another. Repeat to make 2 double bags. Place a heavy weight in the bottom of one bag. This is the bottom bag. Stuff the bag with crumpled newspaper. Glue the second bag inside the top of the first bag. Stuff the second bag with crumpled newspaper. Fold the top of the bag closed and glue. This is the dog's body.

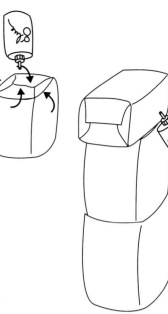

Glue 2 smaller brown paper bags one inside the other. Stuff with crumpled newspaper and glue closed. Glue on top of the body, as shown.

Place the body on top of a piece of cardboard. Trace around the bottom of the bag and draw paws in front, as shown. Cut out. Glue in place under the body for a base.

Glue 3 pieces of brown paper 6 in by 12 in (15cm x 30cm) one on top of another. Draw and cut out 2 ears. Glue them to the head. Glue 2 large brown buttons on the head for eyes, as shown. Use paper eyes if small children are around. Paint and shellac.

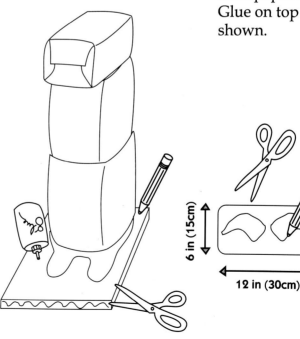

6 in (15cm)

12 in (30cm)

Cat

Spread glue over the outside of a brown paper grocery bag and press inside another bag. Place a heavy weight in the bottom of the bag. Stuff with crumpled newspaper and glue closed. Make another double bag in the same way using 2 lunch bags.

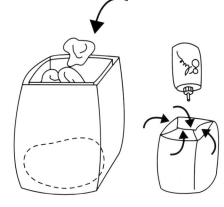

Stuff with crumpled newspaper and glue closed.

Glue the stuffed lunch bag on top of the stuffed grocery bag, as shown.

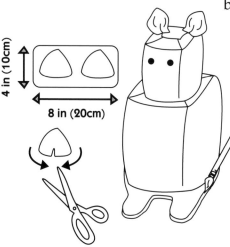

Glue 3 pieces of brown paper 4 in by 8 in (10cm x 20cm) one on top of another. Cut out 2 triangle shapes. Make a 1 in (2.5cm) cut in the center of one side, as shown. Overlap the 2 flaps and glue. Glue the ears to the head, as shown. Paint and shellac.

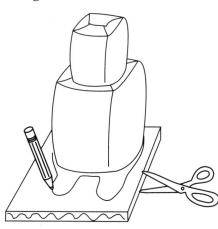

Place the cat body on top of a piece of cardboard. Trace around the bottom of the bag, and draw paws in front, as shown. Cut out. Glue in place under the body for a base.

Mouse

Spread glue over the outside of a lunch bag and press inside another bag. Place a heavy weight in the bottom of the bag. Stuff with crumpled newspaper. Fold opening closed and glue.

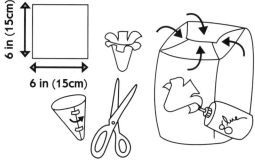

Roll a 6 in (15cm) square of brown paper into a cone and glue. Make 1 in (2.5cm) cuts around the open end of the cone. Glue to the front of the bag, as shown, for mouse nose.

Hoop Rings

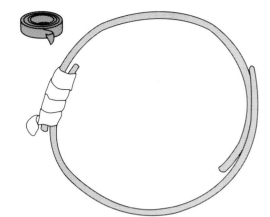

Straighten 2 coat hangers. Bend into a circle large enough to fit easily over the dog. Tape the ends together, as shown.

Drizzle glue over a sheet of newspaper. Twist loosely into a rope, glue side inward.

Wrap the newspaper rope around the wire ring. Make more newspaper ropes to cover the entire ring. Glue the ends down. Make 3 rings for hoop toss game. When dry, paint and shellac.

To play the game, stand each animal in a straight line and far enough apart so a hoop can pass over each animal. Draw a line for child to stand behind. Make it 6 paces from the animals. Child stands behind the line and tries to toss a hoop over each of the animals. Each animal is worth points: 25 points for the dog, 10 points for the cat, and 5 points for the mouse. Keep score for each child and give the winner a prize.

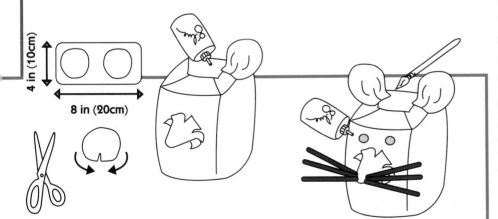

4 in (10cm)

8 in (20cm)

Glue 2 pieces of brown paper 4 in by 8 in (10cm x 20cm) one on top of the other. Cut out 2 mouse ear shapes. Make a 1 in (2.5cm) cut into the center of one side, as shown. Overlap the 2 flaps and glue opening closed.

Glue the ears to the head. Paint and shellac.

Glue 2 buttons for eyes (or use paper eyes) to mouse face. Glue chenille stems to mouse nose for whiskers.

Hide-the-Peanut Game

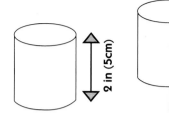

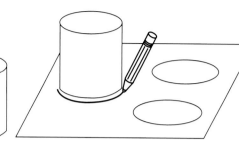

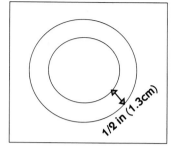

Cut a cardboard tube into 3 pieces each 2 in (5cm) long. Take care to make them exactly the same size.

Place each cylinder on a piece of brown paper and trace around each one.

Draw another circle around the first circle, 1/2 in (1.3cm) larger. Cut out around the larger circle. Do this for each circle drawn.

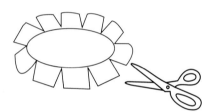

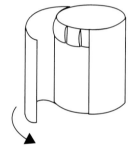

Cut tabs up to the first circle, as shown, on each one.

Put a line of glue around the top edge of each cylinder. Glue one circle onto the end of each cylinder. Fold the tabs down and glue in place.

Cut a piece of brown paper for each cylinder exactly as wide as the cylinder's length and long enough to wrap around it. Glue in place.

Paint all the cylinders exactly alike.

To play the game, place a peanut under one cylinder, line the 3 cylinders in a row. A child quickly moves the 3 cylinders around without lifting them. The other child tries to guess which cylinder the peanut is under.

Gigantic Tulips & Vase

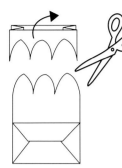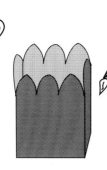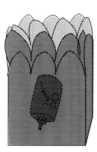

For the tulips, cut around the open ends of 3 medium-size brown paper bags to form petals. Paint inside and out.

Stack and glue these bags together, as shown.

Roll another bag lengthwise into a tight tube. Glue and tape to form a stem. Push the stem into an opening cut in the bottom of the painted bag at the base of the tulip, as shown. Glue and tape in place.

Glue the leaves to the stem. Paint and shellac. Flowers may also be used as theater props.

While the flower is drying, glue 2 layers of brown paper together and cut into strips with a point at each end for leaves.

5 in (12.6cm)

3 in (7.6cm)

For the vase, use a cardboard tube 3 in (7.6cm) in diameter and 5 in (12.6cm) high. Place plastic container inside the tube and cover the outside of the tube with brown paper bag strips or newspaper strips. Glue the paper up to the edge of the plastic container. Paint and shellac. This vase will hold water and can also be used for fresh flowers.

17

Cut-Out Plant Holder

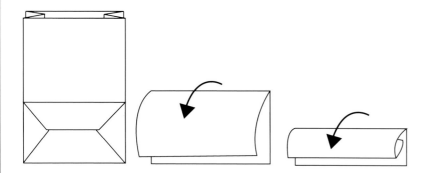

Fold a brown paper lunch bag in half from top to bottom twice.

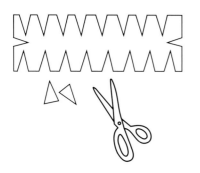

Cut notches in the folded edges.

Open out. Paint and shellac.

Paint another lunch bag in a contrasting color and shellac. Put the uncut bag inside the cut-out bag, and place a potted plant inside the bags. Trim the tops of the bags if they are too tall for the plant.

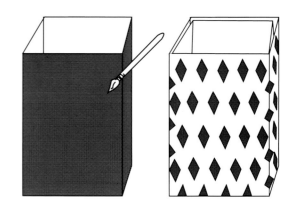

Door Stop

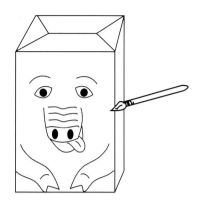

Turn a lunch bag upside down. Paint to resemble a pig, as shown. When dry, shellac.

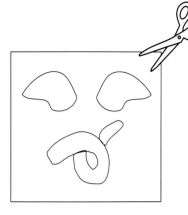

Cut out ears and tail from the side of another brown paper bag.

Paint and shellac the ears. When dry, glue them on, as shown.

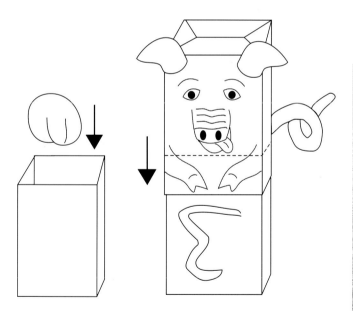

Place a heavy weight in another lunch bag and slide the painted bag over the top. Glue the bags together.

19

Fun on the Farm

Barn

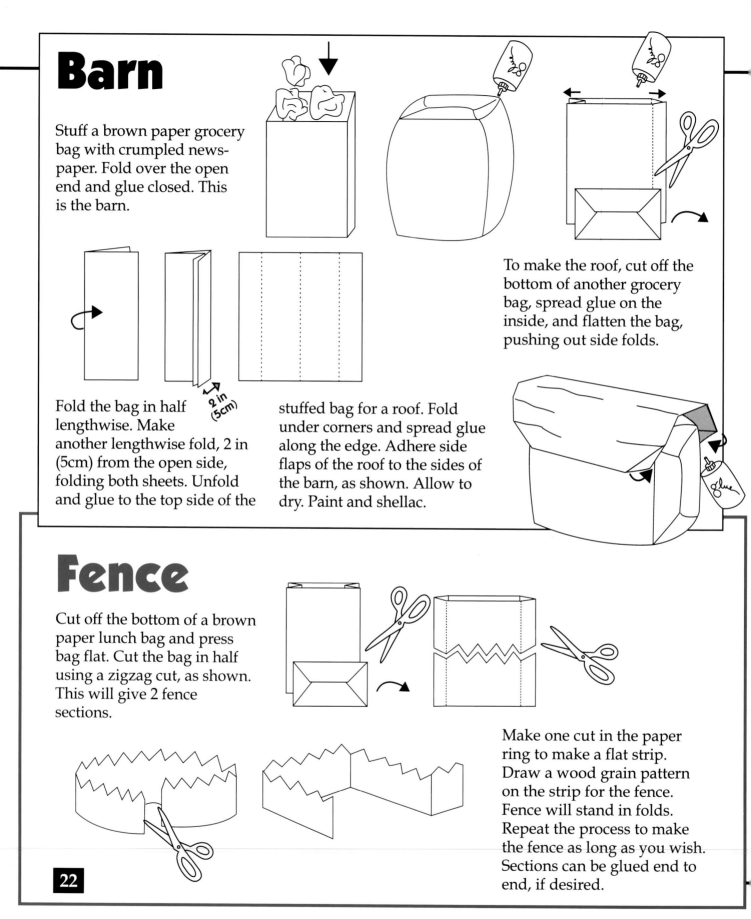

Stuff a brown paper grocery bag with crumpled newspaper. Fold over the open end and glue closed. This is the barn.

Fold the bag in half lengthwise. Make another lengthwise fold, 2 in (5cm) from the open side, folding both sheets. Unfold and glue to the top side of the

2 in (5cm)

stuffed bag for a roof. Fold under corners and spread glue along the edge. Adhere side flaps of the roof to the sides of the barn, as shown. Allow to dry. Paint and shellac.

To make the roof, cut off the bottom of another grocery bag, spread glue on the inside, and flatten the bag, pushing out side folds.

Fence

Cut off the bottom of a brown paper lunch bag and press bag flat. Cut the bag in half using a zigzag cut, as shown. This will give 2 fence sections.

Make one cut in the paper ring to make a flat strip. Draw a wood grain pattern on the strip for the fence. Fence will stand in folds. Repeat the process to make the fence as long as you wish. Sections can be glued end to end, if desired.

22

Chicken Coop

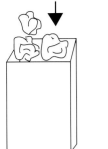

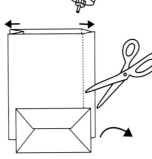

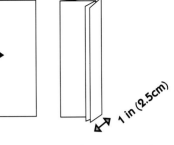

Stuff a brown paper lunch bag with crumpled newspaper. Fold over the open end and glue closed. This is the chicken coop.

To make the roof, cut off the bottom of another lunch bag, spread glue on the inside, and flatten the bag, pushing out side folds.

Fold in half lengthwise. Make another lengthwise fold, 1 in (2.5cm) from open side, as shown.

Glue the paper bag to the top side of the stuffed bag for a roof. Spread glue along the top of the stuffed bag and adhere side flaps of roof to the side of the barn. Allow to dry. Paint and shellac.

Unfold.

Chicken

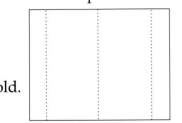

4 in (10cm)   1/2 in (1.3cm)

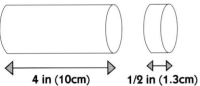

1/2 in (1.3cm)   2 in (5cm)

2 in (5cm)

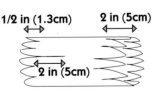

Cut a 4 in (10cm) length from a cardboard tube. Cut another ring 1/2 in (1.3cm) long. Make 2 in (5cm) cuts in one end of the long tube and cut the ends of the cardboard to points. Make 1/2 in (1.3cm) cuts in the other end of the same tube, trimming the ends in the same way. Make another cut 2 in (5cm) long in this same end.

From thin cardboard (cereal box) draw and cut out a chicken head and neck, as shown. Be sure to make it a size to fit the tube body. Insert the neck into the 2 in (5cm) cut in the tube body. Fold the short tabs inward under the head.

Glue the bottom of the chicken to the 1/2 in (1.3cm) ring stand. Paint and shellac.

23

Farmer

Cut a cardboard tube 5-1/2 in (14cm) long. Trace around the end of the tube on brown paper. Measure 1/2 in (1.3cm) wider around the circle. Cut around the larger circle.

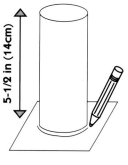

5-1/2 in (14cm)

1/2 in (1.3cm)

Make small cuts in edge of larger circle to smaller circle and glue circle to top of the tube. Fold cut tabs down and glue.

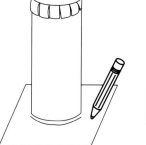

On thin cardboard (cereal box), trace around the other end of the tube. Draw feet sticking out from the circle, as shown. Cut out. Glue to bottom of the tube. On the same cardboard draw arms and a hat brim. Cut out.

With a sharp knife make a cut in the front of the tube 1/2 in (1.3cm) from the top. Insert the hat brim. Glue. Make 2 more cuts at the shoulder area and insert the arms. Glue. Paint and shellac.

Cat

1 in (2.5cm)

Cut a ring from a cardboard tube 1 in (2.5cm) long. On thin, flat cardboard (cereal box), draw and cut out a cat's head and a tail.

Set the ring flat, and glue the head to the front and the tail to the back, as shown. Paint and shellac.

Farm Animals

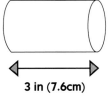

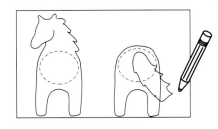

Cut a cardboard tube 3 in (7.6cm) long to make a suitable body for each animal. Place the tube end on thin cardboard (cereal box).

Trace around the tube, lift up and repeat, making 2 circles. Using the circles as the center, draw the head and

front legs on one circle, and a tail and hind legs on the other circle. Cut out and glue to the ends of the tube. Make a pig, cow, horse, dog, using this method. Paint and shellac.

3 in (7.6cm)

Owl

Cut a tube 4 in (10cm) long. Begin cutting 1/2 in (1.3cm) from one end, leaving a 1/2-in (1.3-cm)-wide triangle on each side for ears, as shown. Draw eyes and a beak below the ears. Below the beak, draw a wing on each side of the tube. Starting from the back, cut around the sides of the wings, as shown, leaving the top of the wing attached to the tube. Fold the wings forward. Glue the cut edges at the back bottom end together again. With a sharp knife, cut the bottom 2 sides of the beak, and fold upward. Paint and shellac.

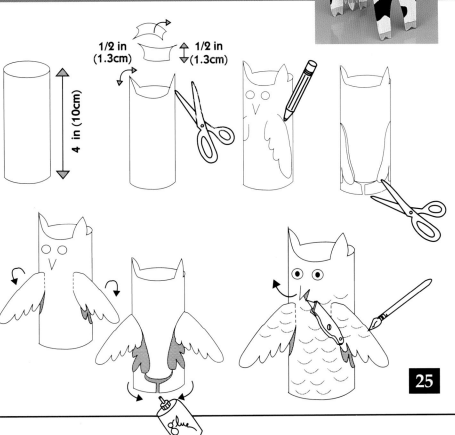

4 in (10cm)

1/2 in (1.3cm) **1/2 in (1.3cm)**

25

Putting on a Show

The Stage

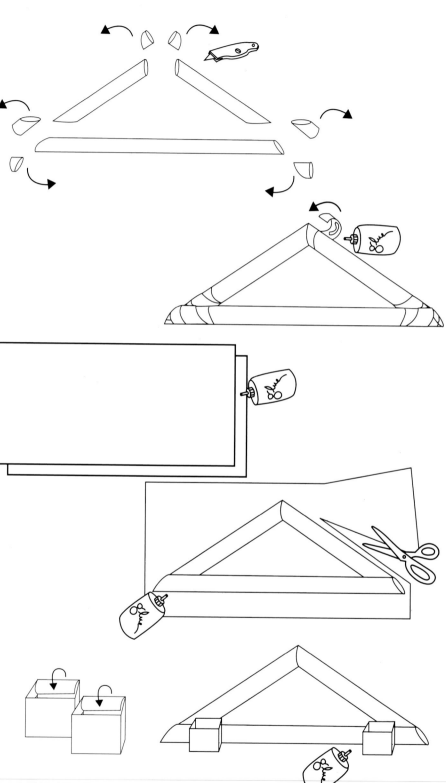

Arrange 3 long cardboard tubes from giftwrap in a triangle. Cut ends at an angle so they will fit together.

Wrap brown paper strips covered with glue around the ends to hold tubes together.

Cut the bottoms out of 2 brown paper grocery bags. Cut down one side and open out to form 2 flat sheets. Spread glue over top of one sheet. Place other sheet on top, and smooth together. Spread glue on back of triangle and place on paper sheet. When glue dries, trim excess paper. Paint triangular tubes gold and back sheet pink and white (see photo p 26-27). This is the pediment.

Fold the ends of a brown paper lunch bag inward to make a shorter bag half as high. Repeat for second bag. Glue one bag to each bottom corner on the back of the triangle, as shown. Weights will go into these bags later for stability.

28

To make pillars, use 10 long cardboard tubes, 5 for each pillar. Glue together, as shown. Hold together with elastic bands until glue dries.

Place 3 double sheets of newspaper one on top of the other, and fold to single sheet size. Fold this in half horizontally, then fold again. Size will be 14 in by 6 in (36cm x 15cm).

Wrap this around one end of one pillar and tape in place. Cut a piece of brown paper 12 in by 14 in (30cm x 36cm). Wrap the brown paper around the newspaper, as shown, with the extra brown paper extending past the end of the tube. Glue in place and fold the excess brown paper in to cover the pillar ends and glue in place. Repeat for second pillar. Paint top of pillar gold and column tubes white.

Cut a toilet tissue tube lengthwise. Cut horizontally into 2-in (5-cm) -wide slices. Trim into leaf shapes. Glue the narrow end to the brown paper front at the top of the pillar, as shown. Tape in place until glue dries. Paint gold.

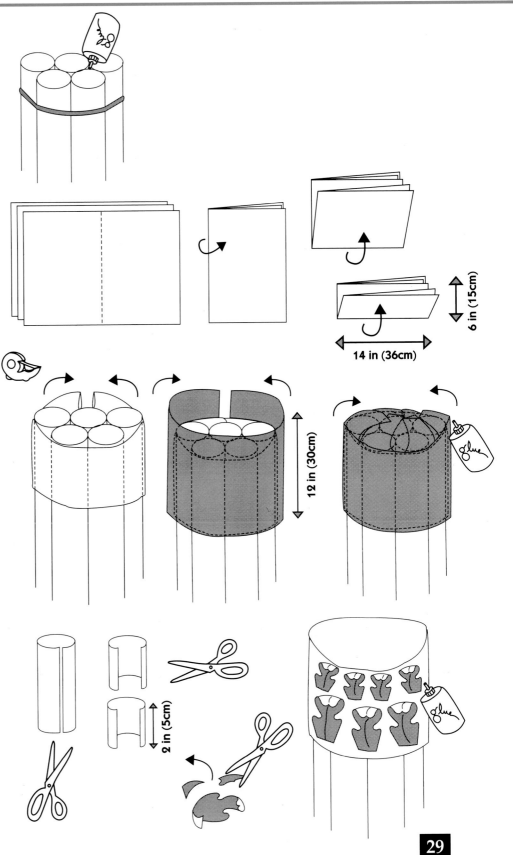

6 in (15cm)

14 in (36cm)

12 in (30cm)

2 in (5cm)

The Stage *continued*

Pillars will also need weights for stability. Fold 2 more lunch bags in the same way as before (p 28), and glue one to the back of each pillar.

To build the stage wings, use 6 brown paper grocery bags, folded flat. Lay them with folded bottoms facing upward. Spread glue on underside of the bottom flaps, adhering them to side of bags. Spread glue in side creases of bags so that bags are glued flat and can't open out.

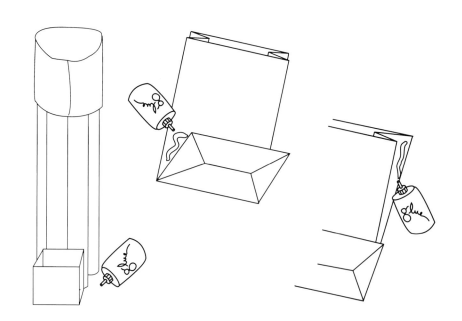

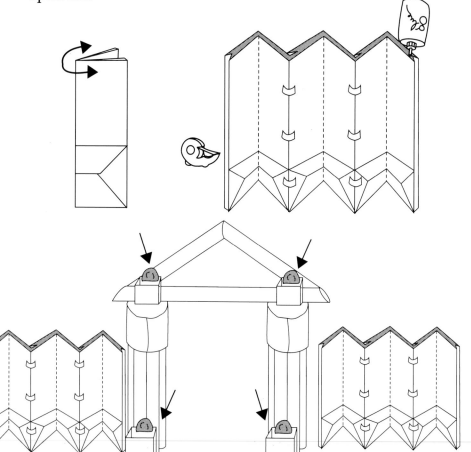

Fold each bag in half, lengthwise. Glue the long edges of 3 bags together to form an accordion shape, as shown. Tape until glue dries. Repeat with other 3 bags. Paint wings pink with white vertical strips on folds to look like more columns (see photo). Shellac.

To assemble, place the the pillars upright, the same distance apart as the width of the pediment. Put a weight in the bags at the back of the pillars. Place the pediment on top of the pillars. Place a weight in each of these bags. Set up the wings on each side of pillars.

King & Queen Tube Puppets

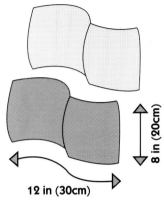

Use 2—14 in (36cm) cardboard tubes as handles for puppets. Cut a piece of crepe paper 12 in long and 8 in wide (30cm x 20cm) for each tube.

14 in (36cm)

8 in (20cm)

12 in (30cm)

Wrap crepe paper around one end of tube and glue in place.

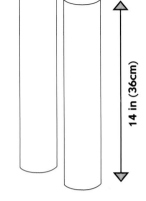

On thin cardboard (cereal box) draw face shapes for a king and queen with crowns and ruffled collars. Cut out.

Glue heads to crepe-paper-covered end of tubes. Paint and add glitter. Make as many other figures as you need for your play, such as a princess, prince, or jester, in the same way.

Flashlight Faces

 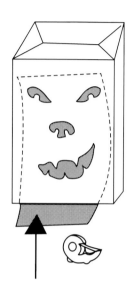 

From the side of a brown paper lunch bag, cut out eyes, nose, mouth, and eyebrows.

Line the front of the bag with colored cellophane or tissue paper.

Put a flashlight in the bag. When you turn on the flashlight the faces will glow.

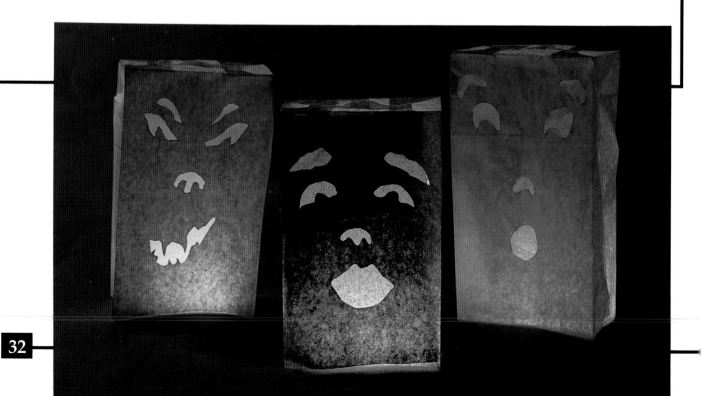

Magic Vest

Cut up the middle of the front of a brown paper grocery bag, until you reach the flat bottom. Cut around the front and 2 sides of the bottom of the bag. Fold the bottom back along one long side. Trim this to the desired collar size.

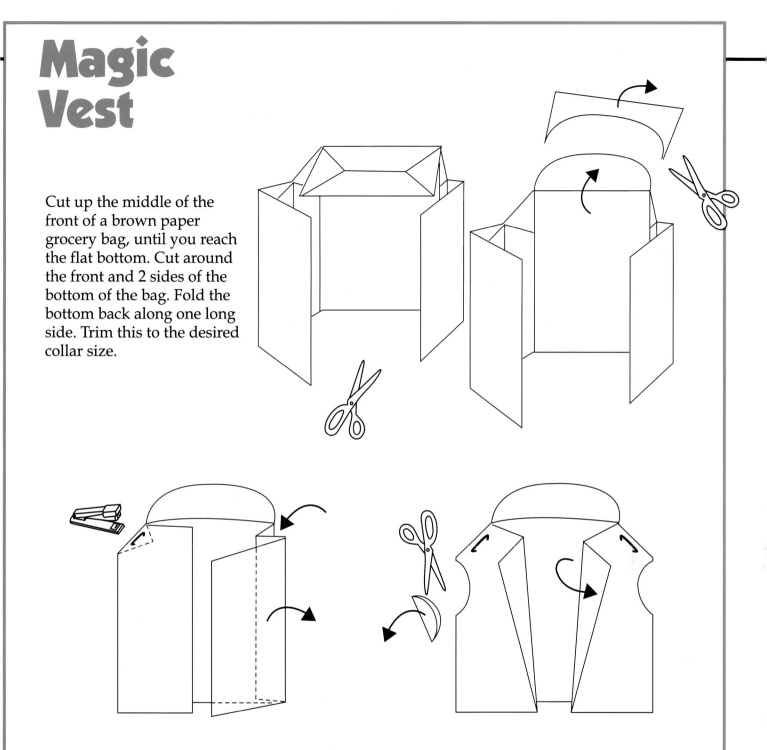

Push out side folds of bag and push in corner folds, as shown, to form shoulders. Staple, as shown.

Cut out 2 armholes from the sides of the bag directly under the shoulder folds. Measure child's arm so it is a comfortable fit.

Fold back 2 lapels at front of vest. Paint and decorate. Shellac.

33

Magic Carpet

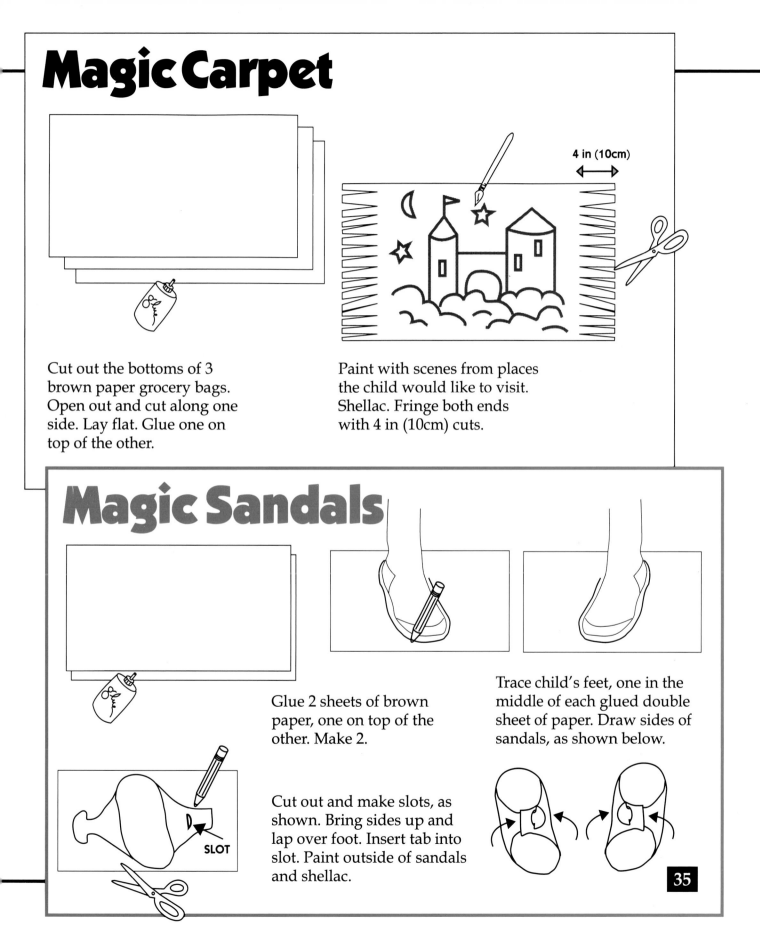

Cut out the bottoms of 3 brown paper grocery bags. Open out and cut along one side. Lay flat. Glue one on top of the other.

Paint with scenes from places the child would like to visit. Shellac. Fringe both ends with 4 in (10cm) cuts.

4 in (10cm)

Magic Sandals

Glue 2 sheets of brown paper, one on top of the other. Make 2.

Trace child's feet, one in the middle of each glued double sheet of paper. Draw sides of sandals, as shown below.

Cut out and make slots, as shown. Bring sides up and lap over foot. Insert tab into slot. Paint outside of sandals and shellac.

SLOT

35

Three Little Pigs

Finger Puppets

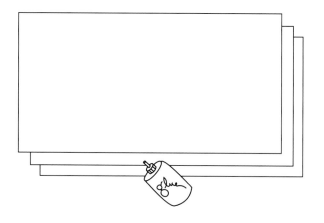

Cut the bottoms out of 3 brown paper grocery bags. Cut down one side and open out to form 3 flat sheets. Spread glue over top of one sheet. Place another sheet on top, and smooth together. Repeat with third sheet to make one strong large sheet.

Draw 3 pig heads, 6 forefeet, 6 hind feet, and 3 tails on the strong large sheet. Cut out. Draw a wolf head, wolf feet, and tail. Cut out.

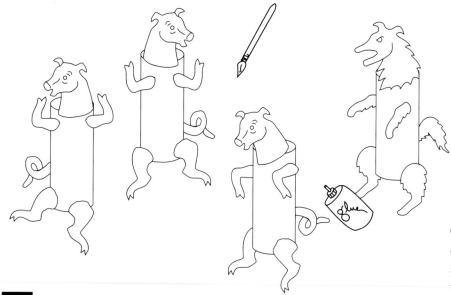

Glue the body parts to the cardboard toilet tissue tubes, as shown. Paint pigs pink and wolf grey and shellac.

Houses

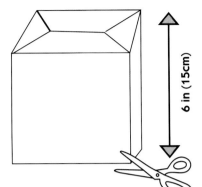

6 in (15cm)

Cut the tops off 3 lunch bags to make them about 6 in (15cm) high. These are the pigs' houses. Turn the bags upside down so that the bags' bottoms become the roofs.

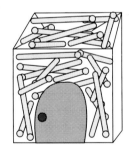

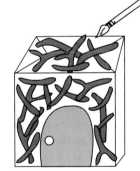

Paint one to look like straw, one to look like sticks, and one a brick pattern. Paint a door on each. Cut around one side, top, and bottom of each door, so puppets can escape the wolf. Use the finger puppets to enact the Three Little Pigs story.

Storage Bag

Decorate a brown paper grocery bag to store the Three Little Pigs puppets and houses when not in use.

THE
THREE
LITTLE
PIGS

Haunted Castle

Haunted Castle

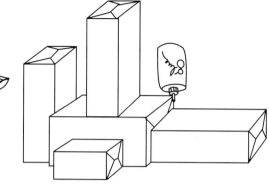

Use 5 brown paper bags in a variety of sizes. Stuff firmly with crumpled newspaper, tape ends shut, and glue bags together to form the parts of the castle. Turrets can be made from long narrow bags.

Draw double arched doors for the entrance and several window shutters on another brown paper bag. Cut out. Paint to look like doors and window shutters, and glue to stuffed bags along one edge of each door or shutter, as shown.

Note: Glue one edge only so the doors and shutters can open.

8 in (20cm)

From another bag, cut 2 circles, each 8 in (20cm) in diameter. Slit from one edge to the center point of each circle. Overlap edges and glue into a cone shape. These are the roofs.

Glue the cone roofs to castle, as shown. Paint openings behind doors and windows black with yellow spooky eyes, which will peer out when shutters are opened. Paint the rest of the castle with black strokes to resemble brick work. Paint window frames and roofs green. Glue castle to a strong cardboard base. When paint is dry, shellac.

Finger Puppets

Stuff a wad of paper towel in one end of a toilet tissue tube and leave a rounded bulge sticking out. This is the ghost's head. Use a sheet of white tissue 13 in by 17 in (33cm x 43cm) and drape it over the ghost's head. Secure around the neck area with a strip of tape. Use scissors to scallop the edges of the tissue, as shown. Paint a face on the head with black paint.

3 in (7.6cm)

1/2 in (1.3cm)

Make a link chain. Cut several strips of brown paper 1/2 in (1.3cm) wide and cut strips into 3 in (7.6cm) lengths. Form first strip into a circle and glue. Link next strip through first strip and glue into a circle. Make chain 6 to 8 links long. For last link cut strip 5 in (12.6cm) long. Place last link around ghost's neck and glue closed.

Make several ghosts in the same way.

43

Harbors
&
Airports

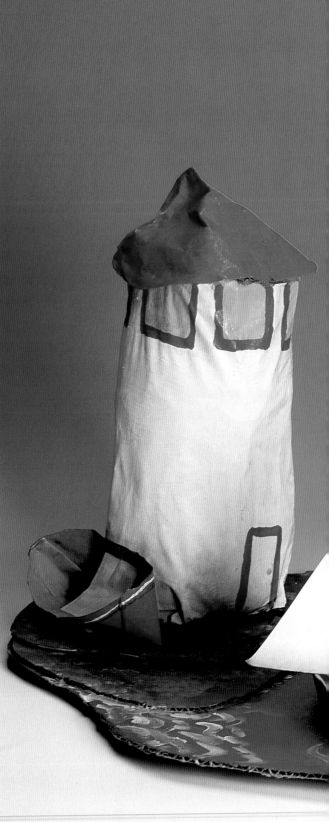

Dock & Buildings at the Harbor

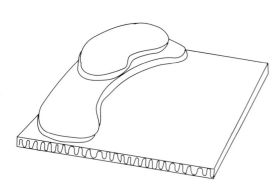

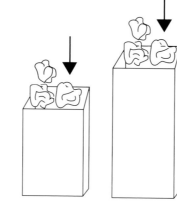

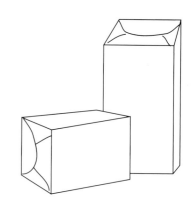

To make water area, open out a cardboard box. Cut out and glue on extra pieces of cardboard from another box to make higher ground.

Stuff a brown paper lunch bag and a long narrow brown paper bag with crumpled newspaper and glue ends shut. Turn the lunch bag on its side and

glue to higher ground area for a warehouse. Set the long narrow bag on end and glue to the higher ground area for the lighthouse.

6 in (15cm)

Cut a 6 in (15cm) circle from another paper bag. Cut from outside edge to center point. Lap over cut edges to make a cone. Glue edges.

Rowboat

Cut a piece of brown paper 6 in by 3 in (15cm x 7.6cm). Make a 1 in (2.5cm) cut in the center of each end, as shown. Overlap the 2 flaps at each end and glue. Glue a seat across the middle. Cut out paper oars. Paint and shellac.

46

6 in (15cm)

1 in (2.5cm)

3 in (7.6cm)

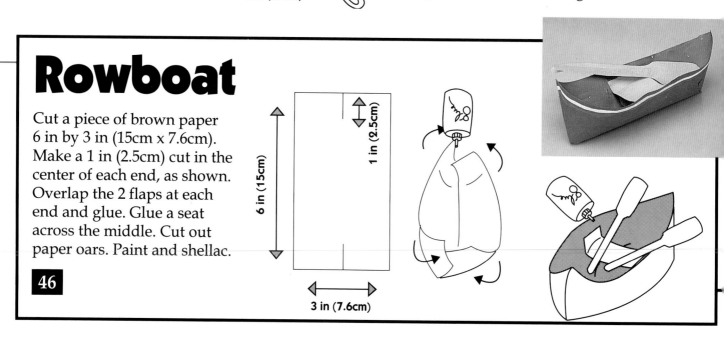

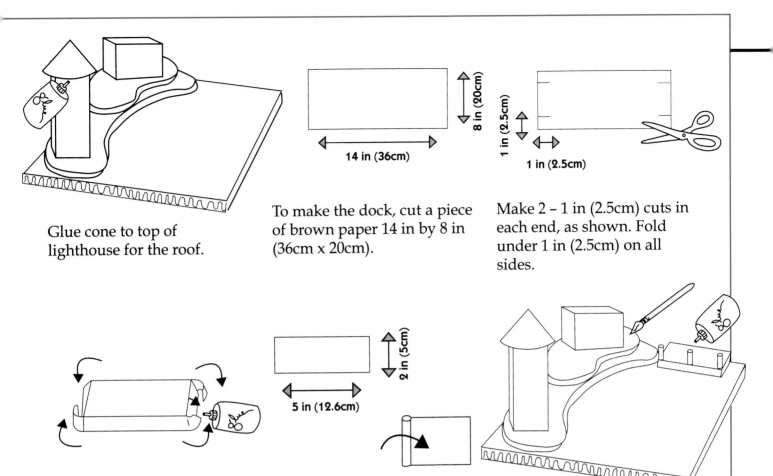

Glue cone to top of lighthouse for the roof.

To make the dock, cut a piece of brown paper 14 in by 8 in (36cm x 20cm).

14 in (36cm)

8 in (20cm)

Make 2 – 1 in (2.5cm) cuts in each end, as shown. Fold under 1 in (2.5cm) on all sides.

1 in (2.5cm)

1 in (2.5cm)

Fold end flaps over and glue in place to make a long open box. Glue in place, open side down, along one edge of the platform bay and touching the land.

Roll up pieces of brown paper 2 in by 5 in (5cm x 12.6cm) into cylinders for posts, as shown. Glue edges and tape. When dry glue along dock to tie up boats.

5 in (12.6cm)

2 in (5cm)

Paint the harbor scene. Allow to dry. Shellac.

Sailboat

Make a rowboat. Then roll up another piece of brown paper 6 in by 3 in (15cm x 7.6cm) into a 6 in (15cm) cylinder for a mast. Glue in center of boat. Cut a sail from another piece of paper 3 in by 4 in (7.6cm x 10cm) and glue on the mast. Paint, as desired. Shellac when paint is dry.

6 in (15cm)

4 in (10cm)

3 in (7.6cm)

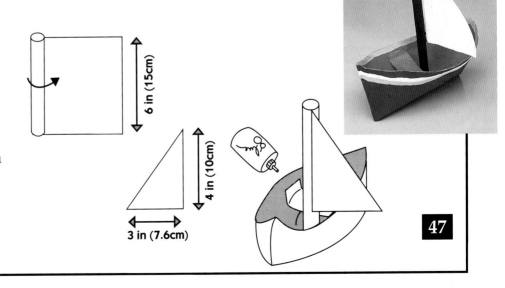

47

Origami Boat

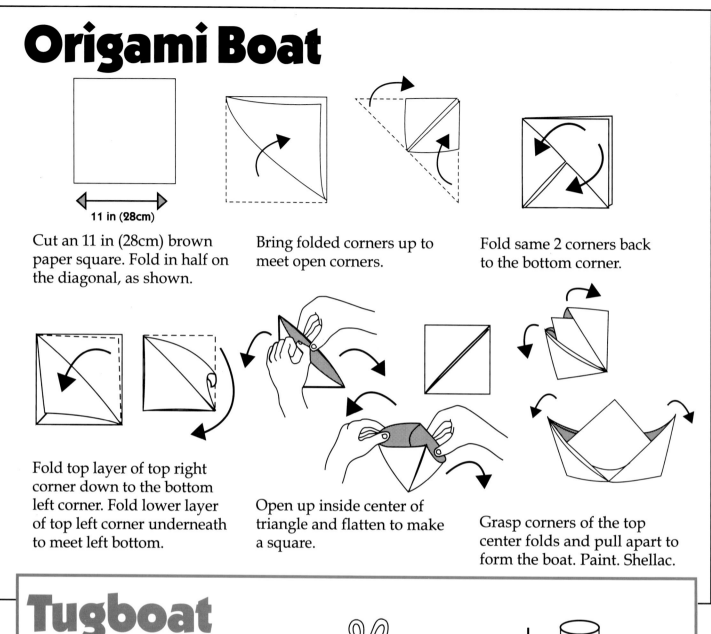

Cut an 11 in (28cm) brown paper square. Fold in half on the diagonal, as shown.

Bring folded corners up to meet open corners.

Fold same 2 corners back to the bottom corner.

Fold top layer of top right corner down to the bottom left corner. Fold lower layer of top left corner underneath to meet left bottom.

Open up inside center of triangle and flatten to make a square.

Grasp corners of the top center folds and pull apart to form the boat. Paint. Shellac.

Tugboat

Make the origami boat. Then make 2 vertical cuts in the center housing of the boat the same distance apart as a cardboard toilet tissue tube is wide. Slide the tube into the cuts and glue the tube in place for a smoke stack. Paint tugboat, as desired. Shellac.

48

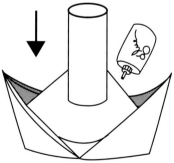

Glue cotton batting on top of the tube for smoke coming from the stack.

Origami Airplane

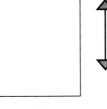

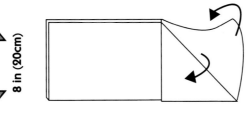

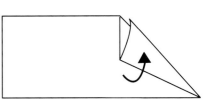

Cut a rectangle 11 in by 8 in (28cm x 20cm) from a brown paper grocery bag or colored sheet of paper.

Fold in half lengthwise. Keep fold at bottom. Fold back corners at one end to meet bottom fold line, as shown.

Then fold these same corners up to meet the diagonal fold, as shown.

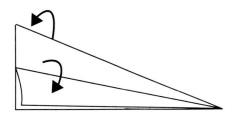

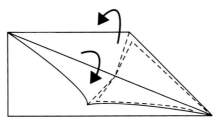

Fold each entire side down diagonally to meet the bottom fold.

Then fold each side down diagonally again to meet bottom fold. Decorate with markers or paint, as desired.

view of plane upside down

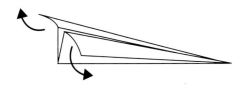

Pull up last fold flap on each side until they are horizontal. Throw airplane forward by gripping the folds underneath. Origami airplane fits inside the hangar on the landing strip (p50).

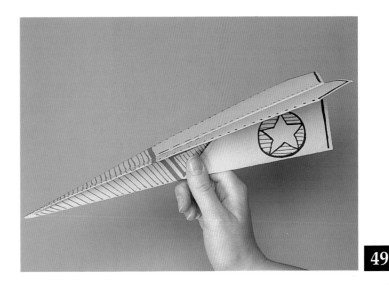

49

Landing Strip

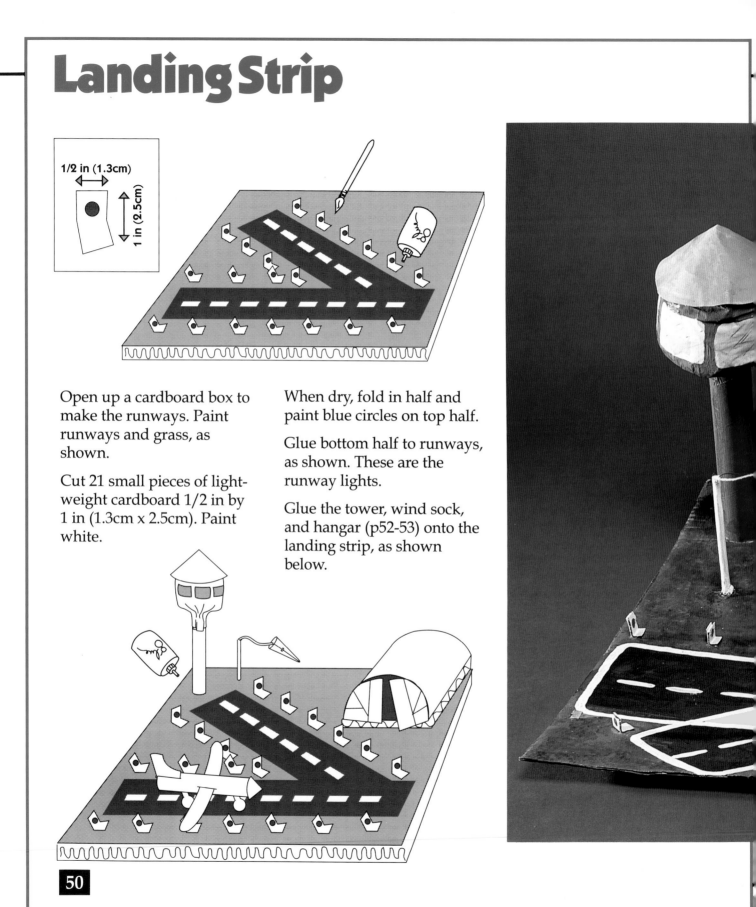

Open up a cardboard box to make the runways. Paint runways and grass, as shown.

Cut 21 small pieces of lightweight cardboard 1/2 in by 1 in (1.3cm x 2.5cm). Paint white.

When dry, fold in half and paint blue circles on top half.

Glue bottom half to runways, as shown. These are the runway lights.

Glue the tower, wind sock, and hangar (p52-53) onto the landing strip, as shown below.

1/2 in (1.3cm)

1 in (2.5cm)

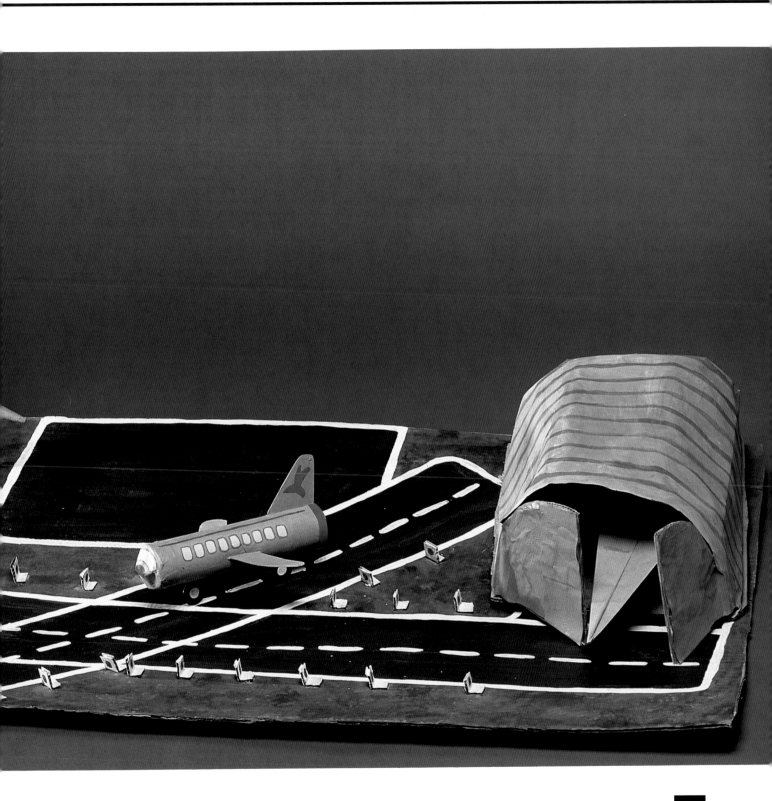

Tower

Insert a 12 in (30cm) cardboard tube into a brown paper lunch bag. Stuff the lunch bag with crumpled newspaper until it is half full. Close the bag around the tube and glue in place.

12 in (30cm)

Cut a circle of brown paper 6 in (15cm) in diameter. Cut from outside edge into center point, as shown. Lap over cut edges to make a cone. Glue closed. This is the tower roof. Glue in place on top of bag, as shown. Paint the tower and add windows all around, as shown. Shellac. Glue to landing strip base (see p50).

6 in (15cm)

Wind Sock

6 in (15cm)

8 in (20cm)

2 in (5cm)

4 in (10cm)

2 in (5cm)

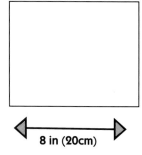

Cut a piece of newspaper 8 in by 6 in (20cm x 15cm).

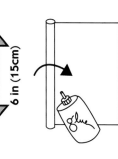 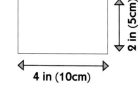

Roll tightly from short end. Glue. Cut another piece of newspaper 2 in by 4 in (5cm x 10cm) and roll to make a small cone.

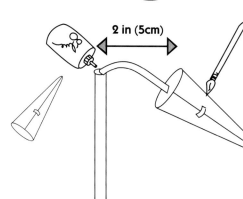

Cut a 2 in (5cm) piece of string. Glue string to open end of cone. Glue other end of string to paper tube. Paint the cone orange. Glue tube to landing strip base (see p50).

Hangar

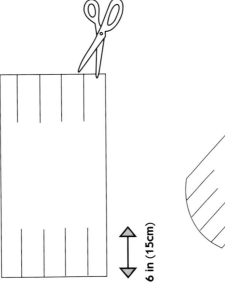

Cut the ends off 2 brown paper bags. Cut to open flat. Glue one on top of the other for strength.

Make 6 in (15cm) cuts in the short ends.

8 in (20cm)

12 in (30cm)

6 in (15cm)

Glue one long side onto a piece of cardboard 8 in by 12 in (20cm x 30cm).

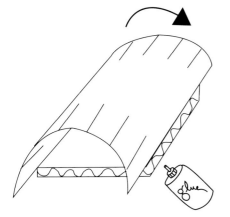

Glue the other side of the paper down to the cardboard to form an arch.

Fold cut tabs down and glue one over the other to form

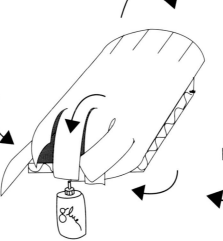

one closed end of the hangar and 2 doors at the other end.

Cut top of doors free so that doors will open. Glue cardboard on back of doors for stability if you wish. Glue to landing strip base (see p50). Paint hangar, as desired. Shellac. Note: If you make several hangars, number them, and color planes to match each hangar, control tower can instruct aircraft on runway.

53

Tube Plane

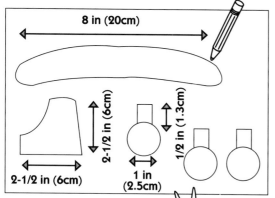

On a piece of firm, thin cardboard (cereal box), draw 3 circles 1 in (2.5cm) in diameter with 1/2 in (1.3cm) tabs at the top of each, as shown, for wheels; a curved wing shape 8 in by 1-1/2 in (20cm x 4cm); and a 2-1/2-in (6-cm) -wedge shape for tail, as shown. Cut out.

Use a cardboard tube 8 in (2cm) long. At the center of the tube, make a cut 1-1/2 in (4cm) long on each side, as shown.

Slide the wing through the cuts at the sides of the tube. Position and glue in place. Make a 2-1/2 in (6cm) cut along the top end of tube, as shown. Slide in the tail piece and glue in place.

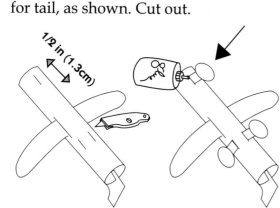

Make 1/2 in (1.3cm) cuts in the under part of the tube, one near the front of the airplane and one on each side near the back. Insert tabs of wheels and glue in place.

Cut a circle 4 in (10cm) in diameter from a brown paper bag. Make a cut from the outside edge to the center point. Lap over the cut edge to make a cone shape and glue. Make 1/2 in (1.3cm) cuts around the edge of the

cone and glue these tabs over the front end of the tube to make the nose for the airplane. Paint and shellac, as desired.

Under the Sea

Fishnet

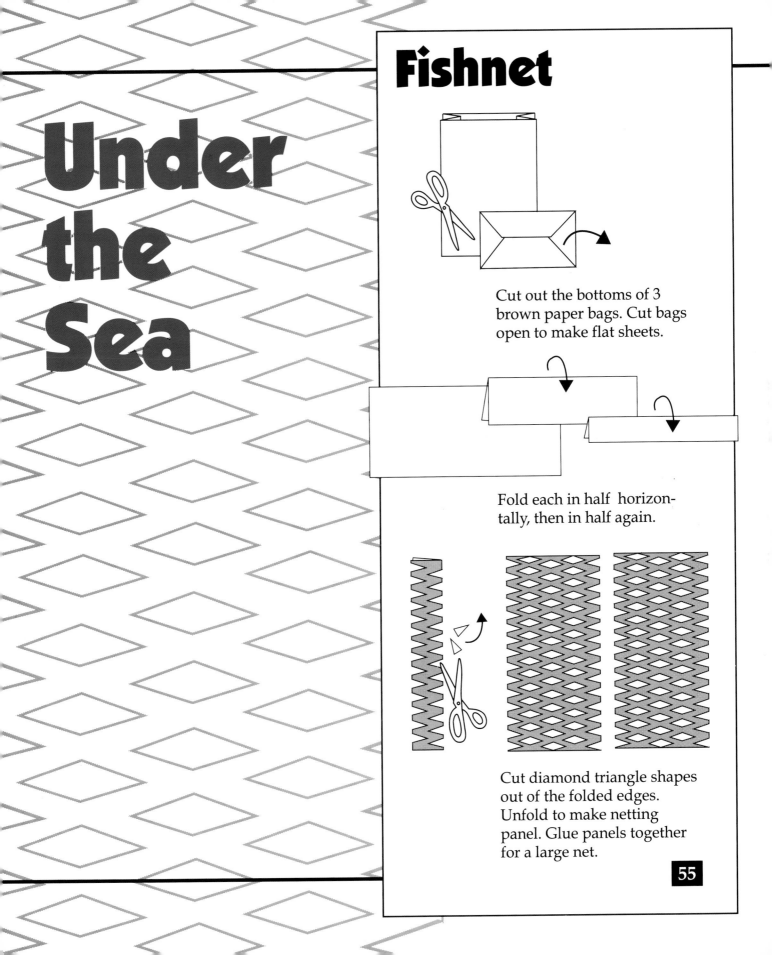

Cut out the bottoms of 3 brown paper bags. Cut bags open to make flat sheets.

Fold each in half horizontally, then in half again.

Cut diamond triangle shapes out of the folded edges. Unfold to make netting panel. Glue panels together for a large net.

Sea Snake

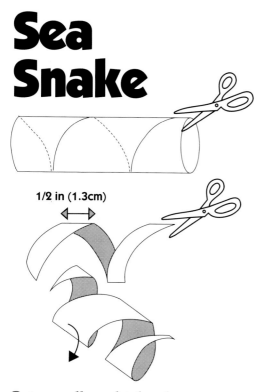

1/2 in (1.3cm)

Cut a cardboard tube along the seam line from end to end, as shown. Make another cut along the same line 1/2 in (1.3cm) away from the first cut, making a curled strip 1/2 in (1.3cm) wide.

Cut one end to form a rounded head. Paint and shellac.

If you wish, color or paint a large sheet of paper for an ocean backdrop. Fish may be suspended in front of backdrop to look as if they are in the water.

Octopus

Stuff a medium-size brown paper bag with crumpled newspaper. Gather open end together and tape closed about 3 in (7.6cm) from the open end.

Cut a large brown paper grocery bag into strips 2 in (5cm) wide. Glue strips together at ends to make strips about 4 ft (120cm) long. Make 16 long strips to make 8 legs.

2 in (5cm)

Place one end of one strip on top of the end of another strip, at right angles. Glue in position.

Fold one strip over the other strip back and forth, maintaining the right angle. Put glue on top fold to close. You have made a catstair. This is one leg of the octopus.

PULL APART

Pull apart the catstair, as shown. Make 7 more catstair legs. Staple the legs to the end of the stuffed paper bag, as shown. Paint to resemble an octopus. Brush paint on outside only of catstair legs.

Suspend from a string glued to the octopus.

Snail

Crumple 4 sheets of newspaper together into a ball. Spread glue over more sheets of newspaper and wrap around the ball until the desired size is reached and the surface is smooth.

Fish

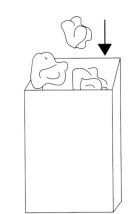

Stuff a brown paper lunch bag with crumpled newspaper. Fold the base of the paper bag inward. Staple at the sides, as shown. This serves as the fish mouth.

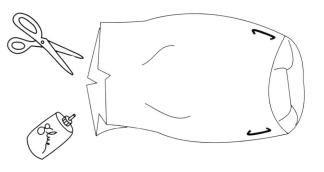

Cut the open end of the bag in a tail shape and glue ends together to the close bag.

Cut out fins from another brown paper bag and glue to the fish body.

Shape the fins and tail with scissors. Paint and shellac the fish. Suspend from a string glued to the fish.

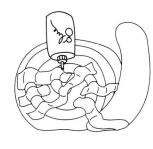
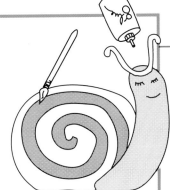

Spread glue over 2 separate sheets of newspaper. Twist one sheet into a long rope. Crumple the other into a rectangle. Glue and tape the rope into a spiral on one side of the ball. Glue and tape the

rectangle to the front of the ball for a body.

When the glue is dry, remove tape, spread glue over small strips of newspaper and smooth the strips over the spiral.

Paint and shellac snail.

Bend a chenille stem into desired shape for antennae. Glue to snail's head, as shown.

Santa's Coming

Reindeer

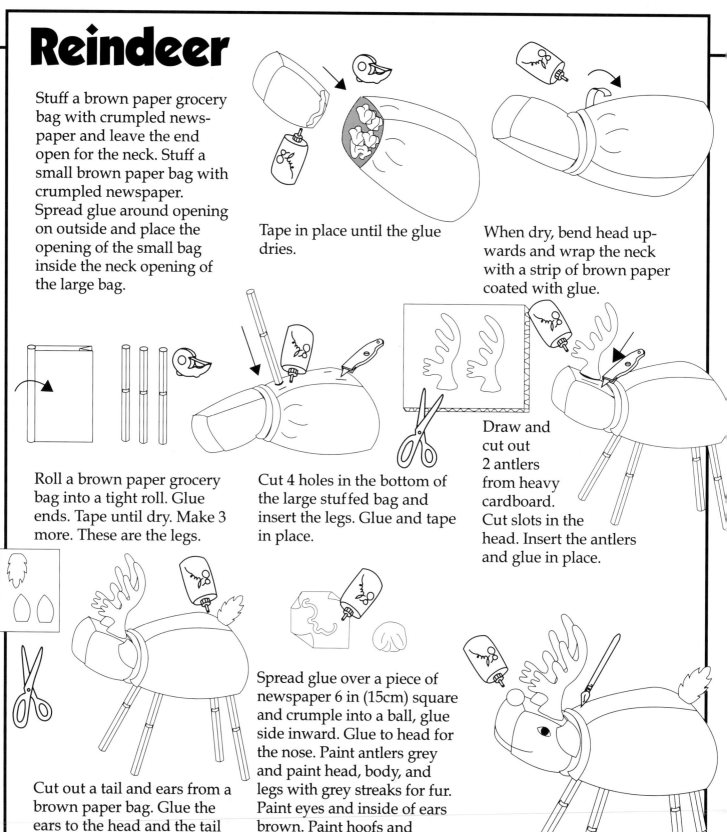

Stuff a brown paper grocery bag with crumpled newspaper and leave the end open for the neck. Stuff a small brown paper bag with crumpled newspaper. Spread glue around opening on outside and place the opening of the small bag inside the neck opening of the large bag.

Tape in place until the glue dries.

When dry, bend head upwards and wrap the neck with a strip of brown paper coated with glue.

Roll a brown paper grocery bag into a tight roll. Glue ends. Tape until dry. Make 3 more. These are the legs.

Cut 4 holes in the bottom of the large stuffed bag and insert the legs. Glue and tape in place.

Draw and cut out 2 antlers from heavy cardboard. Cut slots in the head. Insert the antlers and glue in place.

Cut out a tail and ears from a brown paper bag. Glue the ears to the head and the tail to the body.

Spread glue over a piece of newspaper 6 in (15cm) square and crumple into a ball, glue side inward. Glue to head for the nose. Paint antlers grey and paint head, body, and legs with grey streaks for fur. Paint eyes and inside of ears brown. Paint hoofs and mouth black and nose red. When dry, shellac.

Skates

Draw the pattern for a skate boot without the blade on a folded brown paper bag, placing the bottom of the boot on the inverted "V" fold at one side of the bag. Make 2. Cut out.

Draw and punch 6 lacing boot holes through each side of skate boots. Glue the back of each skate boot together and lace up the front of each skate with yarn, string, or laces. Paint boot design on each boot.

Use a cardboard cereal box to make blades. Draw and cut out the blades and cover with tinfoil.

Glue top of blade inside the "V" fold at the bottom of each skate boot, as shown. These skates may be stuffed from the top with treats for a skating party.

Hammer

Use a cardboard tube 9 in (23cm) long. Cut 2 slits 1 in (2.5cm) deep at opposite sides of one end.

Draw the head of a hammer on thin cardboard (cereal box works well) and cut out. Cover the head with tinfoil.

Put glue on cuts in the tube. Slide the head into the cuts. Allow to dry.

1 in (2.5cm)

9 in (23cm)

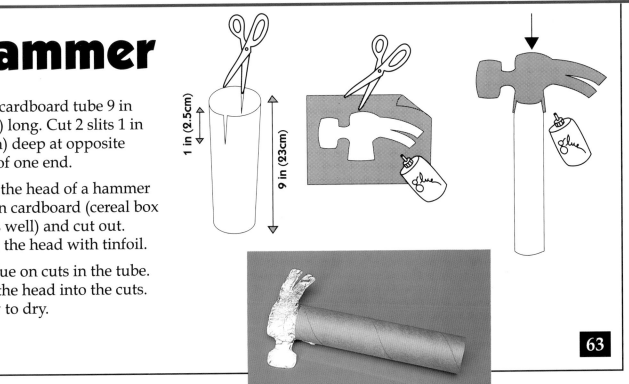

Teddy Bear

Using brown paper bags, make a teddy bear head and body the same as for the doll (p65).

From thick cardboard, draw and cut out 4 legs with paws. Cut out 2 ears and glue to the head. Paint the paws with pink circles. Glue to the body of teddy.

2 in (5cm)

Cut many long strips 2 in (5cm) wide from a brown paper bag. Fringe one side and cut into smaller pieces.

Glue pieces in rows along the body and around the face of teddy for fur.

From thick cardboard, cut out 2 round eyes and 3 small heart shapes for the nose.

Glue the hearts together. Paint the nose pink. Paint the eyes yellow and black.

When dry glue to face. Paint the mouth red with a black outline.

Doll

Stuff a small brown paper bag with crumpled newspaper for a head. Stuff a larger brown paper bag with newspaper for a body. Spread glue around the outside edge of the opening of the small bag. Fit the small bag opening into the large bag opening and hold with tape until glue dries. Reinforce the join with a strip of paper and glue. Allow to dry.

Glue 2 sheets of brown paper together and cut out 2 arms with hands and 2 legs with feet.

Glue the arms near the joined area of the bags and the legs to the bottom of the larger bag. Paint the larger bag to look like a doll's dress.

Use another brown paper bag the same size as the bag used for the head. Cut out the front of the bag. Fringe the bag up from the open edge, all the way around to make a wig. Fringe bangs along the forehead. Glue the inside of the wig bag to the flat part of the head bag. Paint the wig, as desired. Allow to dry.

3 in (7.6cm)

6 in (15cm)

Cut a circle of white paper 6 in (15cm) in diameter to make a collar. Draw a smaller circle 3 in (7.6cm) in diameter inside the larger circle and cut out. Fold larger circle and cut out small pieces of paper to make a lacy pattern. Cut open at the back and wrap

around the neck, overlap and glue in place. Make lace cuffs and pantaloon ruffles from flat oval pieces of white paper, fold, and cut out lacy pattern. Glue to the sleeves and the legs. Cut out brown paper shapes for eyes, nose, and lips. Paint. Glue to face. Shellac.

65

Toboggan

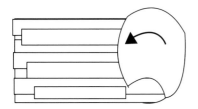

1 in (2.5cm)

Cut the bottoms out of 2 brown paper bags. Cut the bags lengthwise and spread flat. Cut the second bag into 1 in (2.5cm) strips.

Glue the strips, lengthwise, to the first sheet to make slats for the toboggan. Round off one end of the toboggan.

Curl this end by rolling it 3 or 4 times. Clip clothespins on the sides of the roll and allow to dry.

Cut plastic bags into 3 long strips and braid to make a rope for the toboggan.

Poke 2 holes in the curled end of the toboggan. Thread the plastic rope through the holes and knot on the inside.

Draw a figure in winter clothing and a dog or your pet on a heavy brown paper bag. Cut out. Paint to resemble yourself and your pet.

When dry, bend legs and feet of boy and place figures in sitting positions on toboggan. Shellac. Slide toboggan down sofa hill.

Fireplace

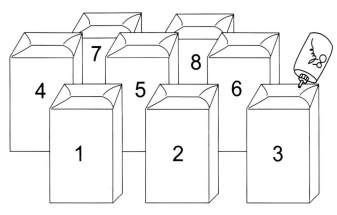

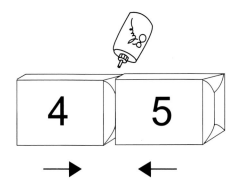

Firmly stuff 8 large brown paper grocery bags with crumpled newspaper.

Fold open ends neatly and glue closed. Number the bags from 1 to 8 at the back.

Glue bags 4 and 5 together end to end, as shown.

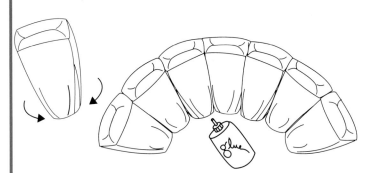

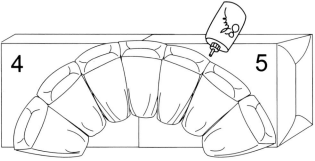

Make an arch by lightly stuffing 7 lunch bags with crumpled newspaper.

Fold ends neatly and glue closed so that the bags are wedge shape, as shown.

Glue sides together with narrow ends on same side to form an arch, and glue to bags 4 and 5.

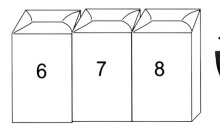

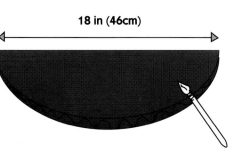

18 in (46cm)

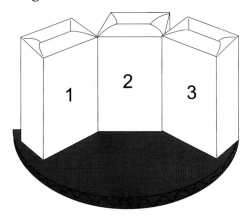

Next glue bags 6, 7, and 8 side by side, as shown. Paint all the bags to resemble stones.
 Allow to dry.

Cut a half circle from firm cardboard 18 in (46cm) wide for the hearth. Paint black. When dry, set bags 1, 2, and 3

around the back of the hearth, as shown. Glue in place, as shown.

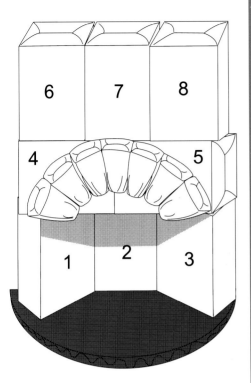

Set bags 4 and 5 on top, across the front, as shown. Set bags 6, 7, and 8 on top of bags 4 and 5, as shown. Tape all sections together at the back with strong tape.

Stockings

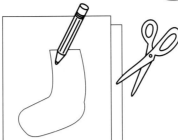

Use 2 pieces of brown paper from a grocery bag that has been cut apart. Lay one on top of the other. Draw a stocking and cut out. You will have 2 stocking pieces.

Glue edges of stocking pieces together, leaving the top open, as shown.

Decorate with cotton balls, buttons, paint, and glitter.

Make as many as you need for your family.

Stuff with surprises. Hang stockings on the fireplace with string or tape to the front, as desired.

Logs

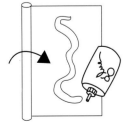

Cut the bottom out of a long brown paper bag. Spread glue on one side. Roll into a tube, glue side inward.

Twist roll tightly. This is one log. Make many logs for the fire.

Cut flame shapes from red and yellow crepe paper.

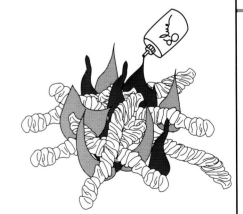

Stack logs and glue crepe paper flames between the logs.

Wreath

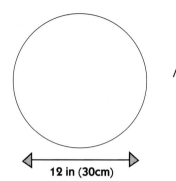

12 in (30cm)

Cut a circle 12 in (30cm) in diameter from a large brown paper bag. Fold in half. Cut a

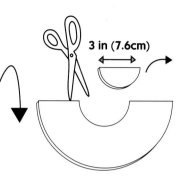

3 in (7.6cm)

half circle from the center of the folded edge 3 in (7.6cm) in diameter, as shown.

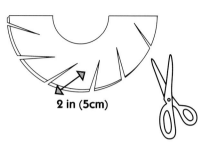

2 in (5cm)

Make angled cuts 2 in (5cm) long around the cut edge of the larger circle, as shown.

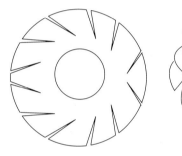

Unfold. Curl alternate cut tabs towards the center of the wreath and glue in place, as shown. Paint.

5 in (12.6cm)

Make pine cones (p74) for the wreath. Make berries from 5 in (12.6cm) brown paper squares. Spread glue on one side of each square and crumple glue side inward. Allow to dry. Make several. Paint red.

8 in (20cm)

2 in (5cm)

3 in (7.6cm)

2 in (5cm)

4 in (10cm)

2 in (5cm)

Make bow from brown paper strip 8 in long by 2 in wide (20cm x 5cm). Fold each end to center and glue. Wrap a 3 in by 2 in (7.6cm x 5cm) strip around center and glue at the

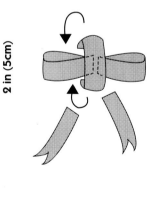

back. Cut 2 strips each 4 in long by 2 in wide (10cm x 5cm). Cut a wedge out of the end of each strip. Glue other ends behind the center of the

bow, as shown. Paint. Glue bow, cones, and berries to wreath. Allow to dry. Shellac.

Christmas Tree

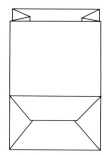

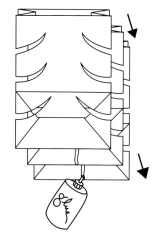

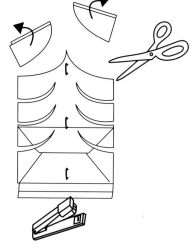

Fold a large brown paper grocery bag in half, vertically. Tree branches are made by cutting diagonal slits along sides, as shown.

Cut 3 more large bags in the same way. Open. Spread glue along folds of bags, as shown. Lay bags one on top of the other with the bases together.

Staple or sew at top, bottom, and center. When dry, stand tree up, paper bag bases at the bottom. Cut the bags to a point at the top, as shown.

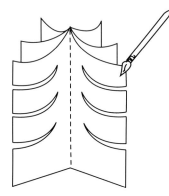

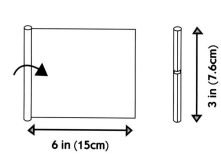

6 in (15cm)

3 in (7.6cm)

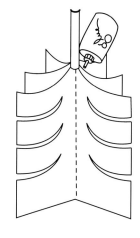

Fan out the branches and spatter with green paint.

Roll a piece of brown paper 6 in long by 3 in wide (15cm x 7.6cm) into a tube 3 in (7.6cm) long.

Glue or staple to the top of the tree. Place the cylinder angel (p73) over the tube and decorate with tree ornaments, pine cones, and cones for candies (p74).

Angel

 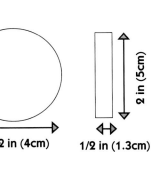 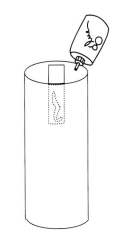 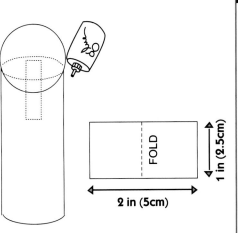

1-1/2 in (4cm)

1/2 in (1.3cm)

2 in (5cm)

FOLD

2 in (5cm)

1 in (2.5cm)

Cover a cardboard toilet tissue tube with foil. Cut a circle of cardboard 1–1/2 in (4cm) in diameter.

Cut a strip of flat thin cardboard 1/2 in wide by 2 in long (1.3cm x 5cm). Glue one end of the strip inside the tube so that 1/2 in (1.3cm) sticks out the top of the tube, as shown.

Glue the circle to the strip so that the circle overlaps the tube, as shown.

Cut a piece of cardboard 2 in long and 1 in wide (5cm x 2.5cm). Fold in half, short ends together, and open again.

Tape in place in front of the angel to resemble a songbook. Paint white.

Glue a paper doily to the back of the tube for angel wings.

When dry, paint black notes on the songbook. Paint an angel face on the circle. Cut hair from gold foil and fringe the ends. Glue to the face, as shown.

Tree Ornaments

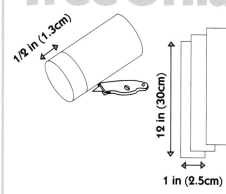

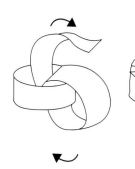

Cut several 1/2 in (1.3cm) rings from toilet tissue tubes. Cut strips of colored crepe paper 1 in wide by 12 in long (2.5cm x 30cm).

Wrap around the rings. Glue ends in place. Hang on tree or decorate some rings with Christmas imagery. On cardboard, draw and cut out a

dove, a star, and a reindeer. Paint. When dry, glue each to a wrapped ring and hang on the tree.

Pine Cones

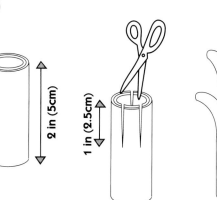

Cut a piece of brown paper bag 2 in wide by 6 in long (5cm x 15cm). Roll into a tube and tape. Make 1 in (2.5cm) cuts at one end. Pull up the center of the tube, like a telescope. Make several. Place pine cones on the tree (p72) or on the wreath (p70).

Cones for Candies

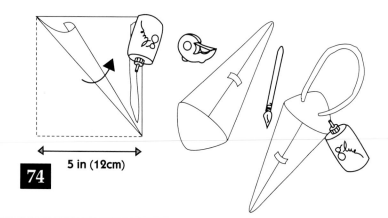

Cut a 5 in (12cm) square of brown paper. Spread glue along one diagonal half and roll (from unglued edge) into a cone, as shown. Tape until dry. Cut a piece of string 5 in (12cm) long and glue ends to open sides of cone to make a hanging loop. Paint, decorate, and fill with candy.

Santa's Sleigh

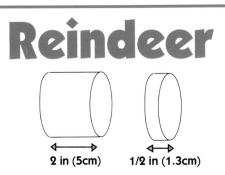

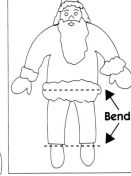

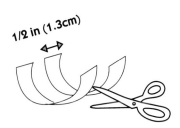

Use a 6 in (15cm) piece from an empty paper towel cardboard tube. Cut the tube from end to end, as shown. Measure 1 in (2.5cm) in from each side of the cut and lightly score the cardboard with a knife. Fold back, as shown. Cut into the ends of the tube to make runners. Cut out curved pieces from one end, as shown. Bend up for sleigh back. Paint grey and brown. Draw or trace a Santa shape on flat thin cardboard, as shown. Cut out and bend at the waist and feet. Glue Santa sitting on the sleigh seat. Paint to resemble Santa Claus.

Reindeer

Cut a 2-in (5-cm) -wide ring from the end of a toilet tissue tube. Cut another ring 1/2 in (1.3cm) wide.

Cut this ring to make 2 half circles, as shown. Put glue in the center of each half circle and glue to the sides of the 2 in (5cm) tube to make legs, as shown.

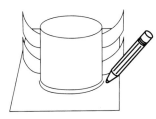

Place the end of the tube on flat thin cardboard (cereal box). Trace around the circle. Draw a reindeer head and neck at the top of one circle, as shown. Cut out. Trace around the tube again to make a second circle. Add a tail and cut out, as shown.

Glue head and tail to the ends of the tube. Paint.

75

Playing House

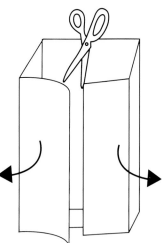

Use 2 brown paper grocery bags for each section of the house. Cut from the opening of the bag, down the middle to the base, and across the base to each side, as shown.

Lay one open bag inside another, open end to base, as shown. Fold the flaps out and over the sides and glue the bags together and flaps down.

Make 2 of these sections and glue together for the house shown. Plan the rooms you want and cut out windows and doors. Make the interior walls from brown paper, glued in place. Paint with latex house paint for extra strength. White latex paint can be tinted with tempra paint for the colors you need.

Miniature dolls to fit in the doll house can be purchased in any toy store.

76

Kitchen Counters

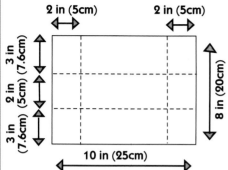

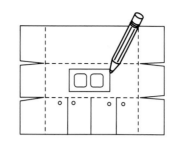

Cut a piece of brown paper 10 in by 8 in (25cm x 20cm). Measure 3 in (7.6cm) margins along the 8 in (20cm) side and 2 in (5cm) along the

10 in (25cm) side and fold. Spread flat. Draw a double sink in the middle section, as shown. Make 2 in (5cm) cuts along 4 folds, as shown.

Fold again, overlap ends, and glue. Paint. When dry, shellac.

Cupboards

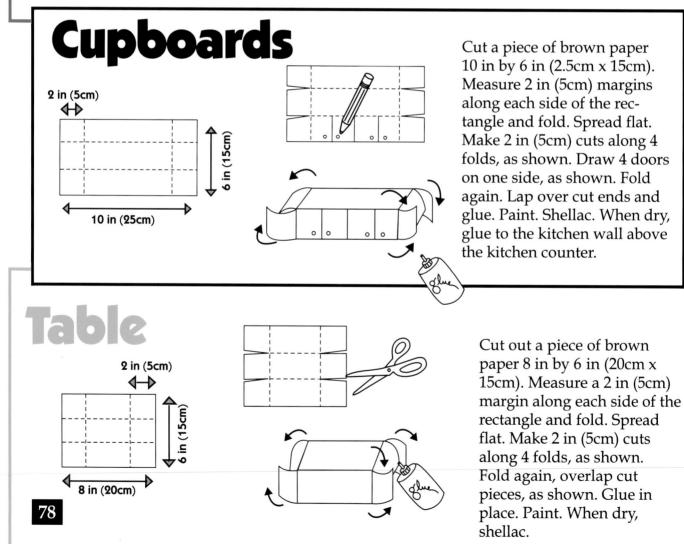

Cut a piece of brown paper 10 in by 6 in (2.5cm x 15cm). Measure 2 in (5cm) margins along each side of the rectangle and fold. Spread flat. Make 2 in (5cm) cuts along 4 folds, as shown. Draw 4 doors on one side, as shown. Fold again. Lap over cut ends and glue. Paint. Shellac. When dry, glue to the kitchen wall above the kitchen counter.

Table

Cut out a piece of brown paper 8 in by 6 in (20cm x 15cm). Measure a 2 in (5cm) margin along each side of the rectangle and fold. Spread flat. Make 2 in (5cm) cuts along 4 folds, as shown. Fold again, overlap cut pieces, as shown. Glue in place. Paint. When dry, shellac.

Refrigerator

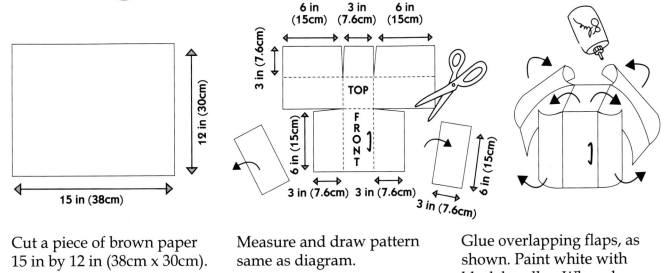

Cut a piece of brown paper 15 in by 12 in (38cm x 30cm).

Measure and draw pattern same as diagram.

Cut where indicated and fold along lines indicated.

Glue overlapping flaps, as shown. Paint white with black handles. When dry, shellac.

Stove

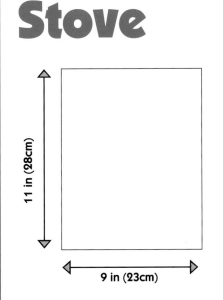

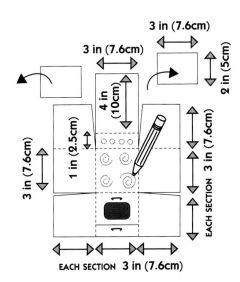

Cut out a piece of brown paper 9 in by 11 in (23cm x 28cm).

Measure and draw pattern same as diagram.

Draw on stove parts. Cut where indicated and fold along lines indicated.

Glue overlapping flaps, as shown. Paint white with black stove parts. When dry, shellac.

79

Chairs

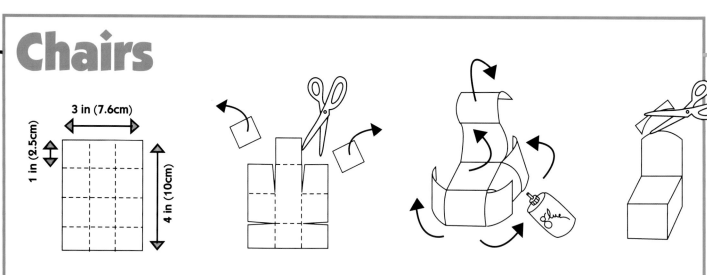

Cut out a piece of brown paper 4 in by 3 in (10cm x 7.6cm). Draw 1 in (2.5cm) squares on the paper, as shown. Fold along all lines.

Make cuts, as indicated. Cut away 2 squares, as shown. Fold pieces, as shown, and glue overlapping flaps, as shown. Fold back of chair up, as shown, and fold back top

half down again and glue for a strong chair back. Cut back of chair into a curve. Use for dining and kitchen tables. Paint chairs to match the appropriate table. Shellac.

Dining Table

Cut out an oval from brown paper 6 in long and 3 in wide (15cm x 7.6cm).

Make 1/2 in (1.3cm) cuts all around the edge of the oval.

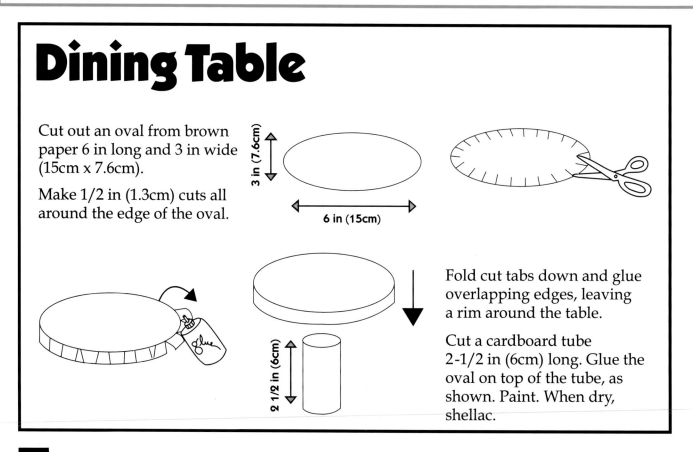

Fold cut tabs down and glue overlapping edges, leaving a rim around the table.

Cut a cardboard tube 2-1/2 in (6cm) long. Glue the oval on top of the tube, as shown. Paint. When dry, shellac.

Living Room Couch

Cut a piece of brown paper 9 in by 10 in (23cm x 25cm). Measure and draw pattern same as diagram.

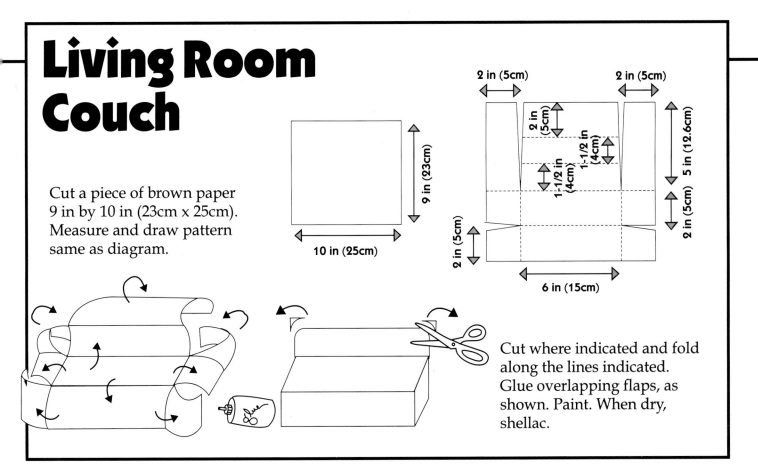

9 in (23cm)

10 in (25cm)

2 in (5cm)   2 in (5cm)

2 in (5cm)

1-1/2 in (4cm)

1-1/2 in (4cm)

5 in (12.6cm)

2 in (5cm)

2 in (5cm)

6 in (15cm)

Cut where indicated and fold along the lines indicated. Glue overlapping flaps, as shown. Paint. When dry, shellac.

Coffee Table

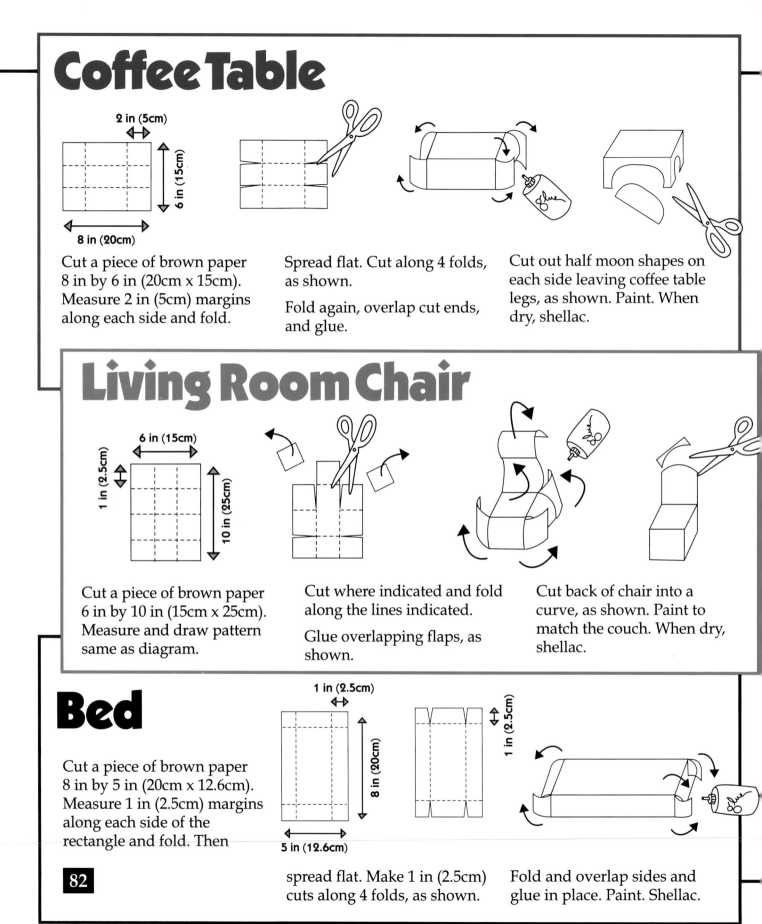

2 in (5cm)

6 in (15cm)

8 in (20cm)

Cut a piece of brown paper 8 in by 6 in (20cm x 15cm). Measure 2 in (5cm) margins along each side and fold.

Spread flat. Cut along 4 folds, as shown.

Fold again, overlap cut ends, and glue.

Cut out half moon shapes on each side leaving coffee table legs, as shown. Paint. When dry, shellac.

Living Room Chair

6 in (15cm)

1 in (2.5cm)

10 in (25cm)

Cut a piece of brown paper 6 in by 10 in (15cm x 25cm). Measure and draw pattern same as diagram.

Cut where indicated and fold along the lines indicated.

Glue overlapping flaps, as shown.

Cut back of chair into a curve, as shown. Paint to match the couch. When dry, shellac.

Bed

Cut a piece of brown paper 8 in by 5 in (20cm x 12.6cm). Measure 1 in (2.5cm) margins along each side of the rectangle and fold. Then

1 in (2.5cm)

8 in (20cm)

5 in (12.6cm)

1 in (2.5cm)

spread flat. Make 1 in (2.5cm) cuts along 4 folds, as shown.

Fold and overlap sides and glue in place. Paint. Shellac.

Pillow

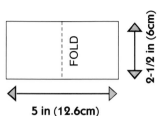
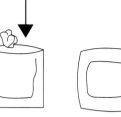

5 in (12.6cm)

2-1/2 in (6cm)

FOLD

Cut a piece of brown paper 5 in by 2-1/2 in (12.6cm x 6cm). Fold in half lengthwise. Glue 2 edges of the pillow

leaving one edge open. When dry, stuff with tiny bits of newspaper. Then glue open end closed. Paint. Shellac.

Bedspread

Cut a piece of brown paper 7 in by 5 in (18cm x 12.6cm). Fold over 1 in (2.5cm) on 3 sides. Paint in a pattern of your choice. When dry, shellac.

Desk with Stool

2 in (5cm)

6 in (15cm)

8 in (20cm)

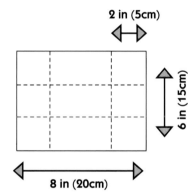

Cut a piece of brown paper 8 in by 6 in (20cm x 15cm). Measure 2 in (5cm) margin along each side of the rectangle and fold. Then spread flat.

On the middle section of one folded side, draw 6 side drawers and a middle drawer, as shown. Cut out a kneehole space under the middle drawer, as shown.

Fold again and overlap sides and glue. Paint. When dry, shellac.

For a desk stool, cut an oval 3 in by 4 in (7.6cm x 10cm) from brown paper. Make 1 in (2.5cm) cuts around the edges. Fold the tabs down and glue overlapping edges in place, as shown. Paint. Shellac.

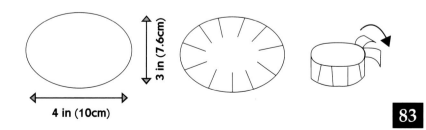

3 in (7.6cm)

4 in (10cm)

Sink

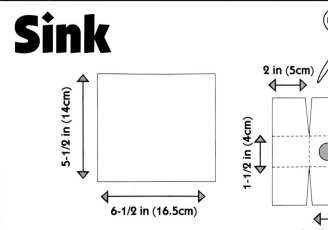

5-1/2 in (14cm)

6-1/2 in (16.5cm)

2 in (5cm) **2 in (5cm)**

1-1/2 in (4cm) **2 in (5cm)** **2 in (5cm)**

2-1/2 in (6cm)

Cut a piece of brown paper 5-1/2 in by 6-1/2 in (14cm x 16.5cm). Measure and draw pattern same as diagram.

Draw a sink in the center panel, as shown. Cut where indicated and fold along the lines indicated.

Glue overlapping flaps, as shown. Paint. When dry, shellac.

Toilet

To make the bowl of the toilet, make another desk stool (p83) and paint white. To make the tank, cut a piece of brown paper 4 in by 5 in (10cm x 12.6cm). Measure and draw pattern same as diagram. Cut and fold along the lines indicated.

1-1/2 in (4cm) **1-1/2 in (4cm)**

1/2 in (1.3cm) **1 1/2 in (4cm)**

1 1/2 in (4cm)

1/2 in (1.3cm) **1/2 in (1.3cm)**

2 in (5cm)

Glue overlapping flaps, as shown. Glue tank on top of one end of bowl, as shown. Paint. When dry, shellac.

Bathtub

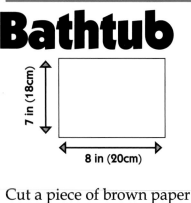

7 in (18cm)

8 in (20cm)

1-1/2 in (4cm) **1-1/2 in (4cm)**

2 in (5cm) **1-1/2 in (4cm)**

1-1/2 in (4cm)

4 in (10cm)

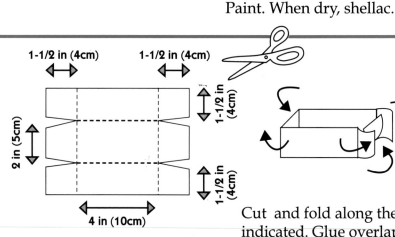

Cut a piece of brown paper 7 in by 8 in (18cm x 20cm).

Measure and draw pattern same as diagram.

Cut and fold along the lines indicated. Glue overlapping flaps, as shown. Paint white. When dry, shellac.

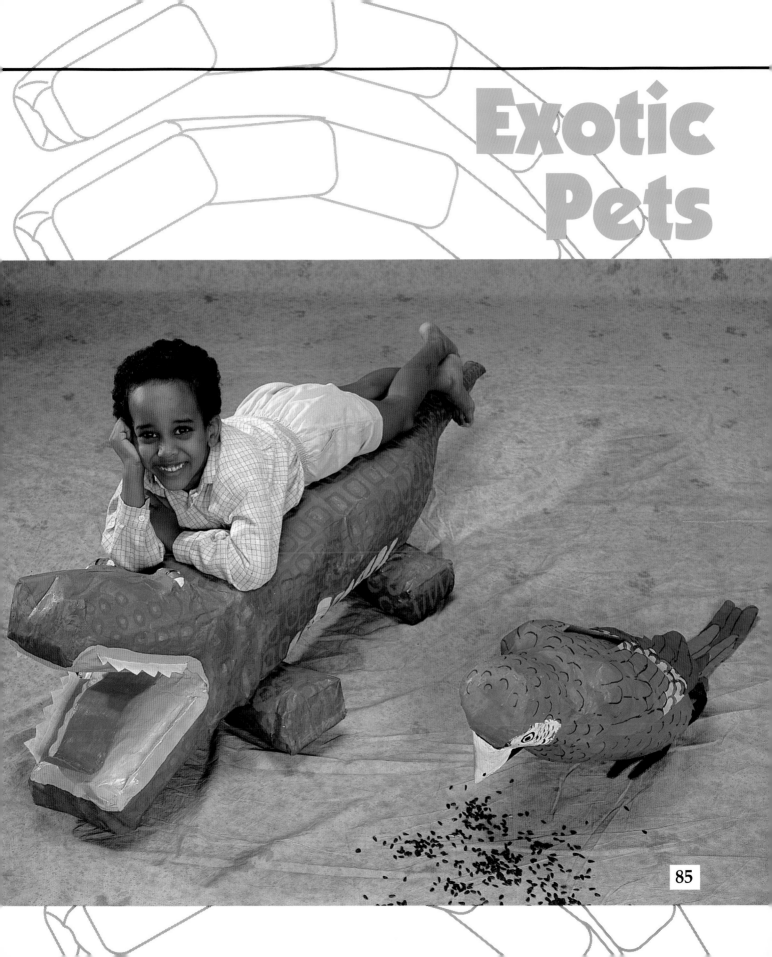

Alligator

Spread glue on the outside of one brown paper grocery bag and smooth inside another to make a double bag. Make 3 double bags.

Stuff one bag with crumpled newspaper. Glue the bottom of the second bag inside the open end of the stuffed bag. Stuff second bag with crumpled newspaper. Attach the third bag in the same way and stuff with crumpled newspaper. Leave the end open. These three bags make the alligator's body.

Make a cut in the middle of each narrow side of another brown paper grocery bag. *Do not cut all the way to the bottom.*

Cut a piece of brown paper as wide as the bag and twice as long. Fold in half lengthwise, and fit into the opening of the bag, as shown. Glue the edges down to make 2 separate bags.

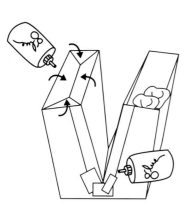

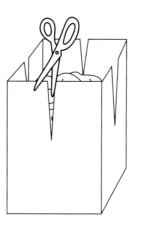

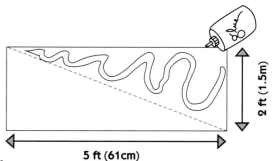

2 ft (1.5m)

5 ft (61cm)

Reinforce the joins and corners with small pieces of brown paper and glue. Stuff the bags with crumpled newspaper. Glue the open ends shut. This is the head.

Cut half way up the middle of each side of another brown paper grocery bag.

Half fill bag with crumpled newspaper.

Cut a piece of brown paper 2 ft by 5 ft (61cm x 1.5m). With pencil and ruler, draw a line from corner to corner, as shown. Spread glue over half of paper. Starting from the unglued corner, roll into a long cone. Dry. Stuff with crumpled newspaper and glue opening closed.

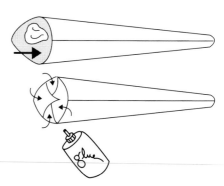

This is the alligator's tail.

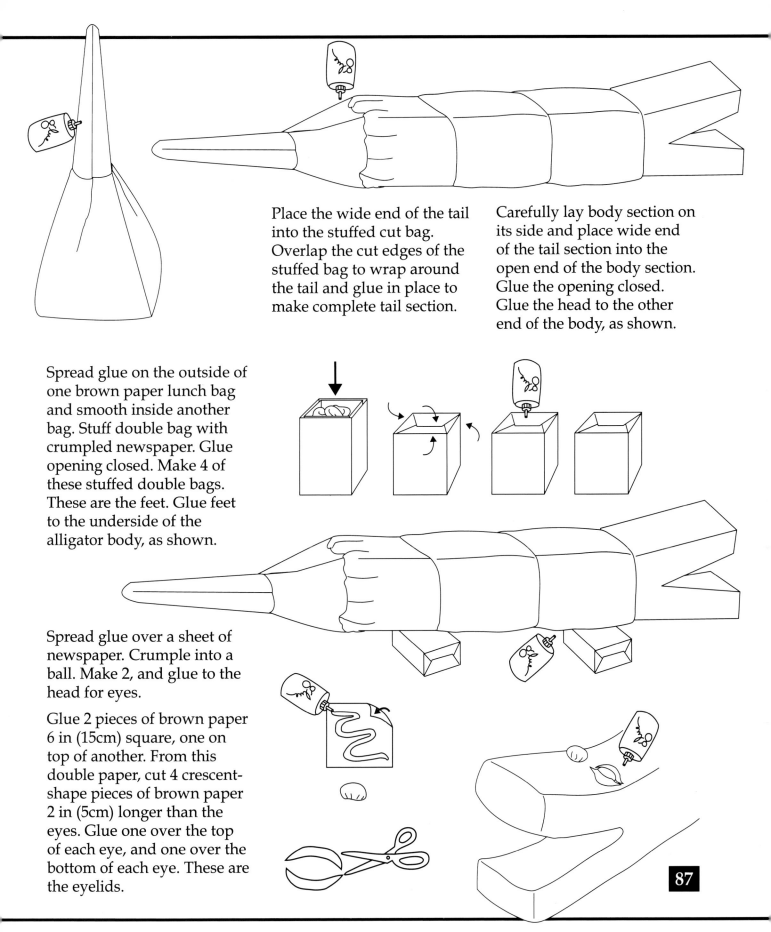

Place the wide end of the tail into the stuffed cut bag. Overlap the cut edges of the stuffed bag to wrap around the tail and glue in place to make complete tail section.

Carefully lay body section on its side and place wide end of the tail section into the open end of the body section. Glue the opening closed. Glue the head to the other end of the body, as shown.

Spread glue on the outside of one brown paper lunch bag and smooth inside another bag. Stuff double bag with crumpled newspaper. Glue opening closed. Make 4 of these stuffed double bags. These are the feet. Glue feet to the underside of the alligator body, as shown.

Spread glue over a sheet of newspaper. Crumple into a ball. Make 2, and glue to the head for eyes.

Glue 2 pieces of brown paper 6 in (15cm) square, one on top of another. From this double paper, cut 4 crescent-shape pieces of brown paper 2 in (5cm) longer than the eyes. Glue one over the top of each eye, and one over the bottom of each eye. These are the eyelids.

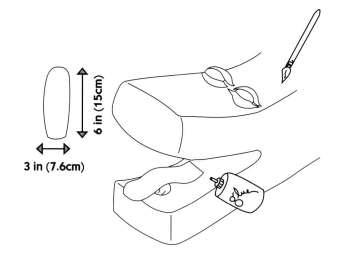

3 in (7.6cm)

6 in (15cm)

Cut 3 pieces of brown paper 6 in by 3 in (15cm x 7.6cm). Glue one on top of another. Round the corners to make a tongue shape. Glue end in place in mouth, as shown. Let tongue curl over a ball of crumpled paper. When dry, remove paper from under tongue.

Paint and shellac the alligator.

Parrot

Cut a large brown paper grocery bag in half lengthwise, dividing the wide side in half, as shown.

Glue one half inside the other to form a tall narrow bag, as shown. Stuff with crumpled newspaper, fold open end closed, and glue.

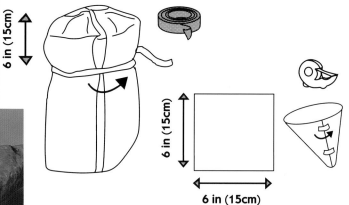

6 in (15cm)

6 in (15cm)

6 in (15cm)

Wrap masking tape around the stuffed bag 6 in (15cm) from the top, and pull tight, forming a neck.

Cut a piece of brown paper 6 in (15cm) square. Roll into a cone and tape.

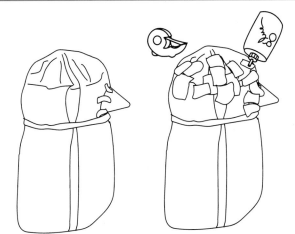

Tape to the front of the head, as shown.

Cut several small pieces of brown paper and glue over the cone joins, tape, and edges of the folded area of the bag.

Open out 3 grocery bags to make flat sheets. Spread glue over one sheet, smooth another sheet over it. Repeat to make a strong triple sheet. Allow to dry.

Draw and cut out 2 wings and a long tail from the triple sheet.

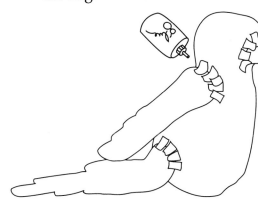

Attach the wings and tail to the body with glue. Cover the attached edges with pieces of brown paper and glue, as shown.

On the side of a cardboard box draw and cut out 2 parrot feet for a base, as shown.

Glue the parrot onto the base, leaning slightly forward. Tape in place until glue dries.

Paint and shellac.

Camel

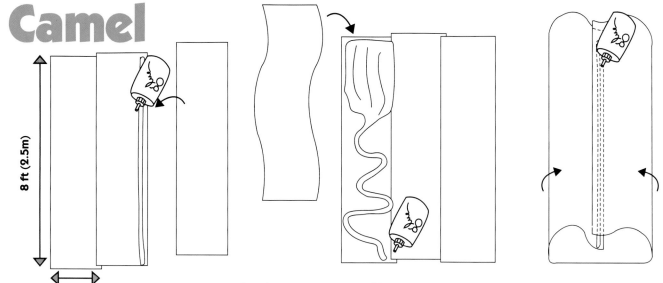

8 ft (2.5m)

2 ft (61cm)

Cut 3 pieces of brown paper, each 8 ft by 2 ft (2.5m x 61cm). Spread glue along the long side of one sheet and attach second sheet to it. Repeat to add the third sheet, as shown.

Cut 3 more pieces of brown paper the same size. Spread glue over one of joined pieces of the first sheet and smooth one of the new pieces over it, as shown. Repeat with the next 2 sheets to form one large, double-thickness sheet.

Bring one long end to the center. Spread glue along the long end. Fold the other long end over and onto the glue.

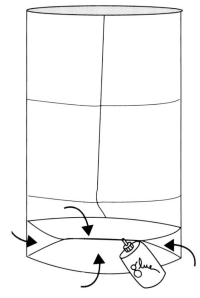

Fold one open end of the paper cylinder closed and glue in place, as shown.

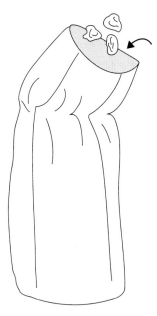

Stuff with crumpled newspaper. When 3/4 full, bend end over, as shown,

and continue to fill with newspaper until full.

Close end and glue shut. This is the camel's body and neck

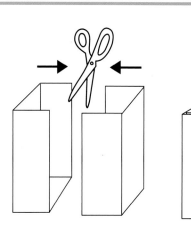

Spread glue on the outside of one brown paper grocery bag and smooth inside another bag. Fill with crumpled newspaper, leave top open.

Cut another grocery bag in half lengthwise, and glue one inside the other, making another narrower bag. Stuff with crumpled newspaper.

Make a 3 in (7.6cm) cut in each side of the open end, as shown. Glue open end shut. Place this bag inside the open end of larger body and neck bag, and glue in place for the head.

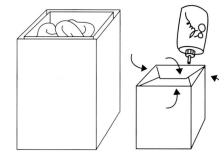
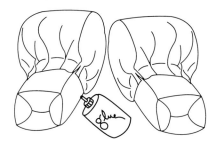

position of back legs

position of front legs

Spread glue on the outside of one grocery bag and smooth inside another. Fill with crumpled newspaper and leave the top open. Glue one lunch bag inside another in the same way and stuff with newspaper. Glue the open end closed.

Place the small stuffed bag inside the open end of the large stuffed grocery bag. Fold opening around small bag and glue in place, as shown. These are camel legs. Make 4 legs in this manner.

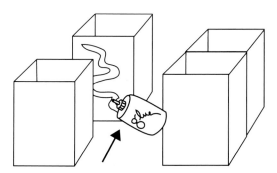

Glue together 2 grocery bags at wide sides, as shown. *Do not stuff.*

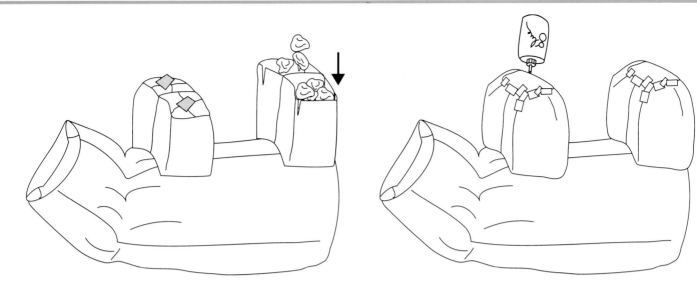

Glue the bottoms of the double bags to the top of the body cylinder, as shown. Make 3 in (7.6cm) vertical cuts in the open ends, as shown.

Stuff with crumpled newspaper. Fold tops closed and tape in place.

Smooth the wrinkles by covering with small pieces of brown paper and glue, as shown. These are camel's humps.

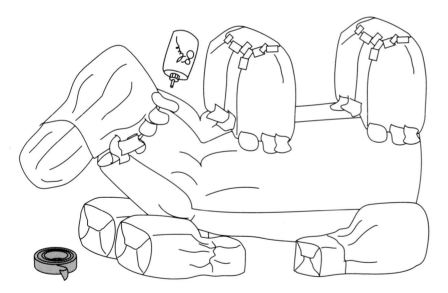

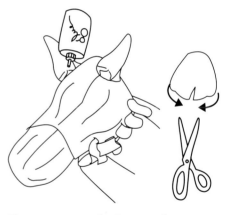

Glue and tape head and legs to body, as shown. Add strips of brown paper and glue to reinforce joins. Support head until dry.

For ears, cut 4 pieces of brown paper 12 in by 12 in (30cm x 30cm). Glue one on top of another. Draw 2 circles 6 in (15cm) in diameter on this piece of strong paper and cut out. Make a 2 in (5cm) cut toward the center of each circle. Overlap cut edges and glue, making a cupped ear, as shown. Glue ears to the top of the camel's head.

1 in (2.5cm)

12 in (30cm)

24 in (61cm)

Cut an oval piece of corrugated cardboard 12 in by 24 in (30cm x 61cm). This is the saddle. Cut long strips of cardboard 1 in (2.5cm) wide for the harness

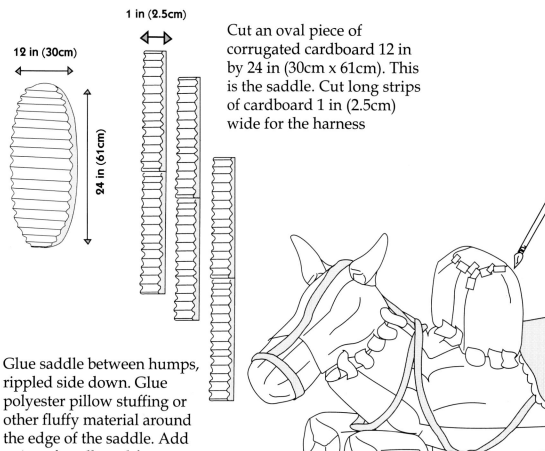

Glue saddle between humps, rippled side down. Glue polyester pillow stuffing or other fluffy material around the edge of the saddle. Add strips of cardboard for harness, as shown. Paint and shellac.

6 in (15cm)

Make 3 tassels from wool. Wrap wool around a 6 in (15cm) piece of cardboard, as shown. When desired thickness is reached, slide looped wool off cardboard.

Wrap and tie a small piece of wool near one end of the loops, trim other end with scissors. Glue tassels to the bridle.

Tiger

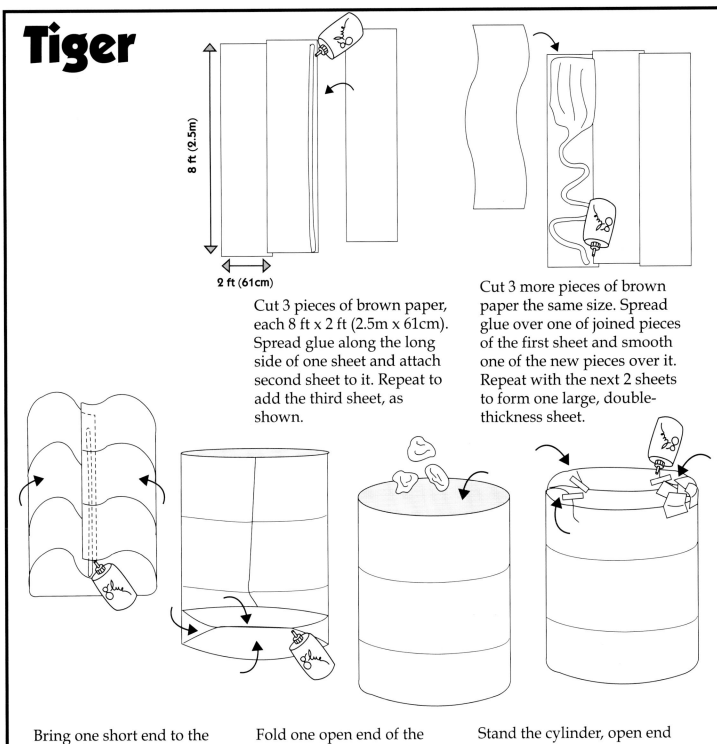

Cut 3 pieces of brown paper, each 8 ft x 2 ft (2.5m x 61cm). Spread glue along the long side of one sheet and attach second sheet to it. Repeat to add the third sheet, as shown.

Cut 3 more pieces of brown paper the same size. Spread glue over one of joined pieces of the first sheet and smooth one of the new pieces over it. Repeat with the next 2 sheets to form one large, double-thickness sheet.

Bring one short end to the center. Spread glue along the short end edge. Fold the other short end over and onto the glue, as shown, to form a cylinder.

Fold one open end of the paper cylinder closed and glue in place, as shown.

Stand the cylinder, open end up. Stuff firmly with crumpled newspaper. Fold over open end and glue closed. Cover the edges and wrinkles with small pieces of brown paper and glue. Allow to dry.

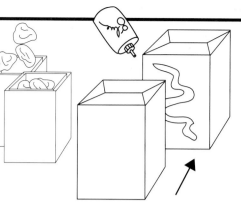

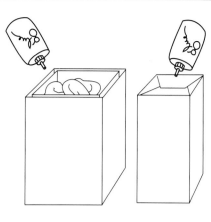

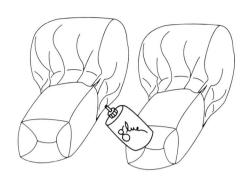

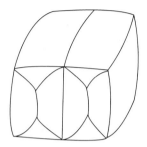

Glue one brown paper grocery bag inside another. Repeat to make 2 double-thickness bags. Fill with crumpled newspaper and glue bags closed.

Glue the 2 grocery bags side by side to form one large block, as shown. This is the tiger's head.

Spread glue on outside of one grocery bag and smooth inside another bag. Fill with crumpled newspaper and leave top open. Glue one long narrow bag inside another bag as before and stuff with newspaper. Glue open end closed.

Place narrow stuffed bag inside open end of larger stuffed grocery bag. Fold opening around narrow bag and glue in place, as shown. This is one hind leg. Repeat process to a make second hind leg.

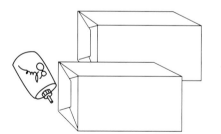

Glue one long narrow bag inside another, stuff with newspaper and glue closed. This is one front leg. Repeat for a second front leg.

Make 6 more double bags as before and fill each bag with crumpled newspaper. Place one bag into open end of another and glue in place. Repeat for all 6 bags, sloping bags for the tail, as shown. Glue open end of the last bag closed.

Lay body cylinder on its side. Glue head, legs, and tail in place, as shown. Secure seams with pieces of brown paper and glue. Allow to dry.

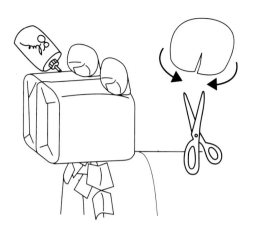

Cut 2 pieces of paper 6 in by 6 in (15cm x 15cm). Glue one on top of another. Repeat. Cut a circle 6 in (15cm) in diameter from each of these pieces. Make a 2 in (5cm) cut toward the center of each circle, as shown. Overlap the cut edges and glue, making 2 cupped ears.

Glue ears to top of head.

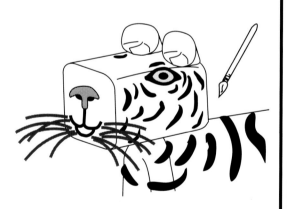

Paint head and body to resemble a tiger. Shellac. Poke small holes in the muzzle area and glue black and white chenille stems in the holes for whiskers.

Penguin

Spread glue on the outside of a brown paper grocery bag and press inside another grocery bag. Repeat to make 2 double bags. Place a heavy weight in the bottom of one bag and stuff with crumpled newspaper. Glue the second bag inside the top of the first. Stuff the second bag with crumpled newspaper. Fold the top of the second bag closed and glue. This is the penguin's body.

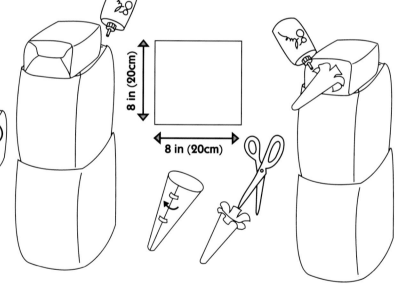

8 in (20cm)

8 in (20cm)

Spread glue on the outside of a lunch bag and press inside another lunch bag. Stuff with crumpled newspaper and glue closed. Glue the stuffed lunch bag on top of the stuffed grocery bag, as shown. This is the head.

Roll an 8 in (20cm) square of paper into a cone and glue. Make 1 in (2.5cm) cuts around the open end of the cone. Glue flaps to front of lunch bag, as shown. This is the penguin's beak.

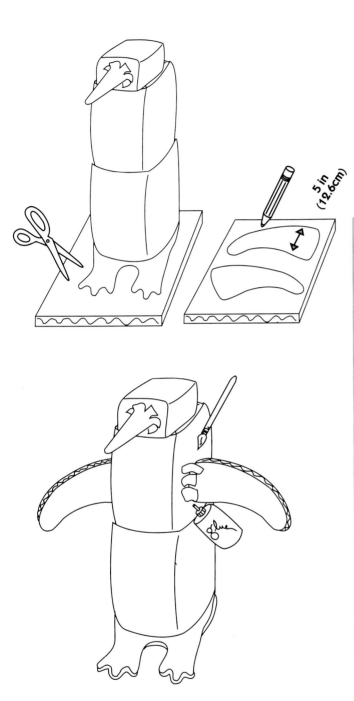

Stand body on top of a piece of cardboard. Trace around the bottom bag and draw feet in front, as shown. Cut out and glue in place under the body for a base.

On a separate piece of cardboard, draw 2 flippers, 12 in (30cm) long and 5 in (12.6cm) wide, as shown.

5 in (12.6cm)

Glue the flippers to the sides of the penguin. Reinforce seams with small pieces of brown paper and glue, as shown. Glue on buttons for eyes, as shown, or use paper eyes. Paint and shellac.

99

Kangaroo

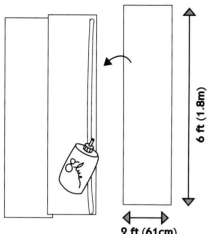 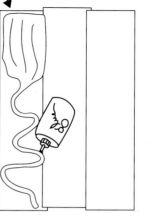 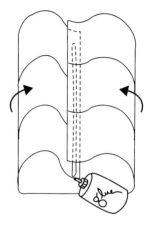

6 ft (1.8m)

2 ft (61cm)

Cut 3 pieces of brown paper, each 6 ft by 2 ft (1.8m x 61cm). Spread glue along the long side edge of one sheet and attach second sheet to it. Repeat to add the third sheet, as shown.

Cut 3 more pieces of brown paper the same size. Spread glue over one of the joined pieces of the first sheet and smooth one of the new pieces over it. Repeat with the next 2 sheets to form one large, double-thickness sheet.

Bring one long side to the center. Spread glue along that side edge. Fold the other long side over and onto the glue, as shown, to form a cylinder.

 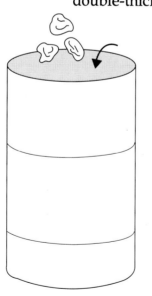 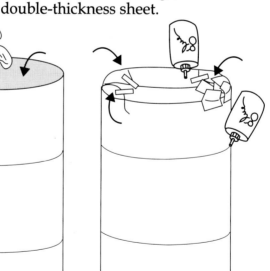 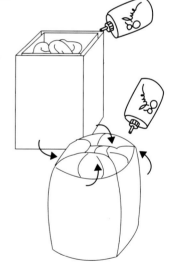

Fold one open end of the paper cylinder closed and glue in place, as shown. Stand the cylinder, open end up. Stuff firmly with crumpled

newspaper. Fold over open end and glue closed. Cover the edges with pieces of brown paper and glue.

For the kangaroo head

spread glue on the outside of one brown paper grocery bag and smooth inside another. Stuff with crumpled newspaper 2/3 full. Make cuts down to the stuffing in the open end. Overlap cut edges of opening and glue shut.

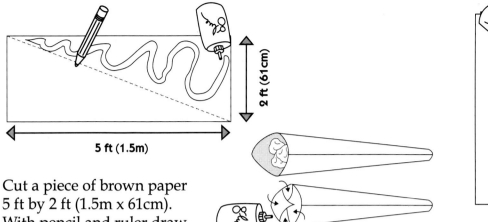

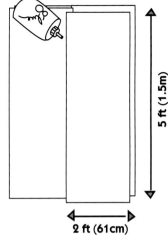

Cut a piece of brown paper 5 ft by 2 ft (1.5m x 61cm). With pencil and ruler draw a line from one corner to the opposite corner, as shown. Spread glue over one side of this line and roll paper, starting at opposite corner, to

make a cone. Stuff with crumpled newspaper. Glue open end closed. This is the kangaroo's tail.

Cut 4 pieces of brown paper 2 ft by 5 ft (61cm x 1.5m). Spread glue along the long side of one sheet and attach second sheet to it, as shown. Glue the other 2 pieces of brown paper in the same way.

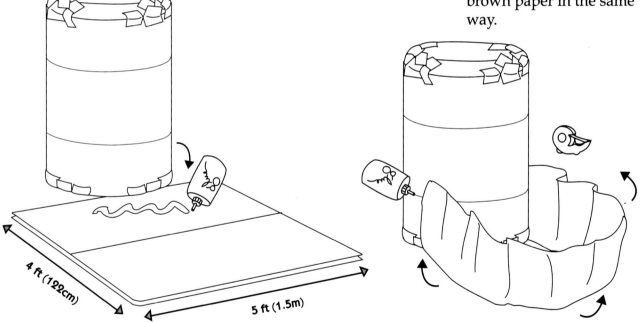

Spread glue over one joined sheet and smooth second joined sheet over it to form one large, double-thickness sheet. Spread glue at the

102

center of the 5 ft (1.5m) side of this sheet. Place the body cylinder on this glue, as shown.

Fold the sides of the flat sheet up and attach the ends to the sides of the cylinder with glue. Make pleats in the sheet and glue and tape in place. This forms a pouch in front of the cylinder.

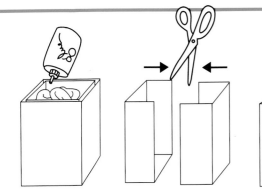

Spread glue on the outside of one grocery bag and smooth inside another. Fill with crumpled newspaper and leave top open. Cut one grocery bag in half lengthwise and glue one inside the other making a long narrow

bag. Stuff with crumpled newspaper. Glue open end closed.

Place narrow stuffed bag inside open end of the larger stuffed grocery bag. Fold opening around narrow bag and glue in place. This is one

hind leg. Repeat to make second hind leg.

For front leg, glue one narrow bag inside another. Lightly stuff with newspaper and glue closed. Make 2. Bend the ends of the front legs over, as shown.

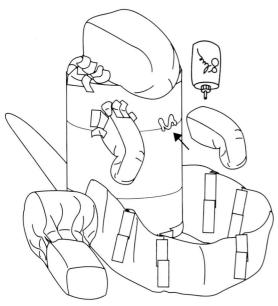

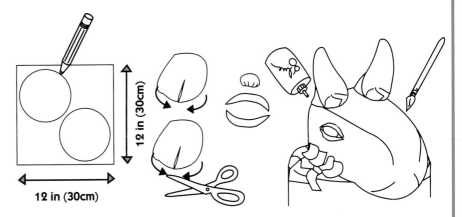

Glue hind legs, front legs, tail, and head in place, as shown. Add pieces of brown paper and glue to reinforce the attached parts.

To make ears, cut 4 pieces of brown paper into 12 in (30cm) squares. Glue one on top of another. Draw 2 circles 6 in (15cm) in diameter and cut out. Make a 2 in (5cm) cut toward the center of each circle. Overlap cut edges and glue, making a cupped ear. Glue ears to the top of kangaroo's head.

Spread glue over a sheet of newspaper. Crumple into a ball. Make 2, and glue to the head for eyes.

Cut 4 crescent-shape pieces of brown paper 2 in (5cm) longer than the eyes. Glue one over the top of each eye, and one over the bottom of each eye. These are eyelids.

Paint and shellac the kangaroo.

103

Index